Spoken Thoughts from an Amalgamated Advocate in Today's America: (Political, Social, and Civic Reflections from a Dedicated American)

Foreward: A Written Set of Thoughts Concerning the Author of "Spoken Thoughts"…by Jason Johnson, Ph.D.

Why Spoken Thoughts?

SPEECHES: The Spoken Thoughts

I0454735

1. *Lenny McAllister, Atlanta Tea Party 1-year anniversary: 2010 Feb 27* ("Mandating American Exceptionalism") *- page 14*
2. *Ghostwritten: RNC July 2009 (NAACP) - 1st Draft: 2009 June 28* (The Bond and The Dream) *– page 25*
3. *Lenny McAllister, MLK Day Celebration in Ocala, FL - 2010 January 18* ("MLK Day, Furthering The Dream of Yesterday, and Waking Up for a Better Future")*- page 42*
4. *Lenny McAllister, Ocala Tea Party - 2010 January 18* ("Martin Luther King Was a Tea Party Patriot") *- page 48*
5. *Lenny McAllister, Carolina Sweet Tea Party - 2009 April 3* ("Social Responsibility and American Ambassadors") *- page 61*
6. *Lenny McAllister, Bainbridge, GA: 2010 April 15* ("The TEA Party Must Mean More than Just Taxed Enough Already") *- page 68*
7. *Lenny McAllister, Illinois Tax Day Revolt: 2011 April 15* ("A Party for Touting Exceptionalism in America") *- page 78*
8. *Lenny McAllister, 4th of July Celebration Event: 2009 July 4* ("From C to C to C") *- page 92*
9. *Lenny McAllister, Take Back Our State Tea Party: 2009 June 3* ("Wall") *- page 104*
10. *Lenny McAllister, 2010 July 26 (Republican Party of Lee County / Speaker Series) (Ernest and Ruby McSwain*

Agriculture Center) ("Conviction for the 3 Rs during Today's Teachable Moment"*) - **page 108**

11. *Lenny McAllister, Albany, GA / SWGA Patriots: 2010 April 17 (*"Taking Back America, Taking Back Americanism"*) - **page 122***

12. *Lenny McAllister, Springfield, MO / Americans for Prosperity: 2012 July 21 (**Fearing American Competition, Failing in Applying American Capitalism, and Falling Short as Free-Market Advocates**)- **page 134***

13. *Lenny McAllister: 2012 Peoria Tax Day Tea Party: 2012 April 17 (*"A New Beginning, A New Hope, and A Better Change"*) - **page 146***

14. *Lenny McAllister: Rally for Common Sense, 2012 May 19 (*"Convert The Masses, Don't Preach to the Choir"*) - **page 161***

OP-EDs: The Written Thoughts

15. Fighting for Choice While Eliminating Choices – **page 171**
16. We Are The Change – **page 174**
17. A Pound of Hubris when an Ounce of Humility Would Do – **page 177**
18. Challenging the NAACP, Condemning the Tea Party Express, yet Confronting the Truth on Contemporary Racism – **page 182**
19. Harvesting Strange Fruits – **page 186**
20. Misguided Priorities while "Fighting Misogyny" - **page 190**
21. Sins of the Father, Part 2: Why We Have to Act Now – **page 194**
22. What's This Generation's Emmett Till's Moment?- **page 197**
23. The Meaning for the 4th of July for Today's… - **page 202**
24. The Obama PASS (Presidential Activism Selectively Shown)- **page 208**
25. Drinking the Kool-Aid While Sipping the Tea- **page 212**

26. Cain, Conservatism and the Black Vote for 2012 and Beyond – *page 217*
27. The Trayvon Gap Between Civil Rights Leaders and the Political Right – *page 221*

Looking Forward: Why I Stay Amalgamated - Politics as a Life or Death Sport that Remains a Part of the Game of Life

A Written Set of Thoughts Concerning the Author of "Spoken Thoughts"

When it comes to political commentators you have two types. There are those who are true believers, men and women who advocate for the policies of one party, speak the talking points of its main candidates and do their best to make sure the Democrats or the Republicans stay in power. Then you have the cynics. Those are men and women who do not truly believe much of what they are saying, but they know full well that spouting nonsense on television or radio will make them famous and quotable and lead to more pundit power. What you are about to read are the words of a true believer, and ideologue and a man of amazing conviction and faith, which means you are about to read one of the rarest books on the market.

In the African-American political commentary community, there are ideologues and cynics as well. There are also a plethora of gadflies, charlatans and hustlers that are all steadily crawling all over each other to get that rare two minute clip on CNN, MSNBC or Fox that they can parlay into a book deal, a speaking tour or that most elusive of awards: the television contributor contract. Opportunities to speak about critical issues of the day are rare for African-Americans so there is always the temptation to do something outlandish to make yourself stand out. Things like: getting into volatile arguments with other guests; shucking and jiving for the majority audience; or worse, proudly calling yourself a Hip-Hop Republican during the peak of Obama-Mania in the presidential election of 2008.

Enter Lenny McAllister.

I met Lenny at the 2008 Republican convention, in a felt chair on the second floor of the Xcel Energy Center in Minneapolis typing on his lap-top with one hand and juggling a cell phone with the other. I had seen him before on CNN and I was convinced he was a cynical opportunist. There are plenty of African-American Republican voters, despite what the popular press may lead you to believe. However, calling yourself a Hip-Hop Republican? I was sure Mr. McAllister was just trying to fill a demographic gap in the punditocracy and would fall back on empty GOP talking points the moment he was challenged. It would not be the first time I mis-judged and under-estimated Lenny McAllister.

It started off slowly. Random texts during the debates, brief conversations during the Sunday morning talk shows. Eventually text messages were replaced by appearing on air together, arguing about policy but then going out for coffee afterwards. As time went on, Lenny and I discussed his political evolution, why he believed in the principles of the Republican Party, his own struggles to transform the party from within, and his personal commitment to the success and advancement of African-American youth. Coffees transformed into late night strategy discussions as I finished my PhD and Lenny discussed his passion to finish his education. When I discussed the political minefield that is academic politics, he would vent about trying to lift the racial cataracts off the eyes of the Republican Party. I invited him to speak at my college; he invited me to be on his show in Chicago. Bit by bit, I began to learn about a complex life story that was almost twice as interesting as the political beliefs of the man who lived it. In short, while I never agree with his politics, I learned that this self-deprecating, humorous and passionate man was the real deal. In short, I learned that Lenny McAllister is not a Republican out of convenience, or spite, or cynical branding; he is a Republican because, at his core, he is a man who believes in the power of individual agency. Lenny McAllister is a Republican because he has lived the life that would break most people, has not even reached the promise land yet, but is not about to give up on the glory that will be his to experience when he does it by his own work ethic.

The speeches you are about to read may not make you vote for the Grand Old Party or make you send a donation to the Heritage Foundation but they will give you something that is so much more. In every page through every letter you will get a glimpse into that rarest of prisms. The heart and mind of a sincere, committed God-fearing political ideologue. You will get to see something that I did not believe existed until befriending Lenny McAllister: that an African-American man, with depth, with intelligence, with moral credibility, and with not a drop of cynicism can be a proud, card-carrying member of the Republican Party. Enjoy every page of this book and share these thoughts and works with your friends and relatives. I do not believe there are any books like this out on the market, because I sincerely believe there is not anyone else like Lenny out there.

....Jason Johnson, Ph. D., author of *Political Consultants and Campaigns: One Day to Sell* (Westview Press, 2011)

Why "Spoken Thoughts"?

Yes, I get it. And yes, I understand your question:

Why "Spoken Thoughts"?

Of course, it is likely that you're asking the question not only about the title of the book – why in the world would I name this book "Spoken Thoughts from an Amalgamated Advocate in Today's America: (Political, Social, and Civic Reflections from a Dedicated American)" – but you're also wondering why would I feel the need to put my spoken thoughts down onto paper, in a book no less?

Well, thoughts are powerful. Usually, we don't get a chance to see what people are thinking. I wanted to bring a little change to that.

Yes, we get a chance to see what people will do based on what they are thinking. Sometimes that has disastrous results attached to it. Sometimes, people's actions – whether their pure actions actually have a legitimate tie to twisted thoughts or vice versa – end up being a mere representation of what they "thought" they were thinking. In a world of multiple social media tools, various outlets for expression, and a 24-hour society, it seems as though people have less of a capacity to express a thought with the resonance and foresight to spark action past emotion. Even when people speak what they are thinking – and they are able to do that in the purest sense – the vast majority of the time, they are speaking what they are feeling, not thinking.

Again, with "Spoken Thoughts", I wanted to bring a little change to that.

Not everyone can be at a speech. Even if one had a chance to attend one of these events where the speeches of this book were given, one probably didn't have the chance to take in everything that I wanted to say. To be truthful, sometimes I didn't get a chance to say everything that was on my heart. Sometimes I found myself veering off of the transcript based on the reaction of the crowd or a conversation that I might have had before going on stage. As I continued to give public addresses, though, I realized that the reason why I wrote up my comments was not to "follow the script" or be safe.

I wanted to be focused. If possible, I wanted to teach a point while at the lectern. I wanted to have a distinct, cogent, and direct message with my words. That's the responsibility of a public speaker, in my opinion. Plenty of people – and we have seen this (sadly) within the Tea Party Movement over the past 4 years – can grab a microphone, recite some talking points, and yell their disgust for a group of elected officials and other leaders. That is not statesmanship. That is not leadership. That is not worthwhile to me or, in my view, to our nation. It just isn't. And because that is how I feel, I always want to make sure that I come to the lectern with a different feel, a distinct message, and a defined belief that we can impact American politics – and dare I say, the American society – with a higher standard of effort and decorum to improve the nation.

To me, it's hard to really believe that or act in that fashion without the power of thought guiding the way.

Or, perhaps, spoken thoughts.

The purpose of putting those thoughts onto paper – in this instance, speeches and articles – is for you to get a better idea of what drives me as a child of God, as a Black American, and as a Christian Republican. Perhaps this set of writings will not give you the whole story, nor should it. I don't believe that the whole of any individual can be captured in a few writings sprinkled over the course of several months or even a few years. We as children of God are so much more complex than just the amalgamation of a few thoughts, characteristics, or experiences.

And yet, that combination can be a gateway to a litany of thoughts and actions, and perhaps even become a spark for a revolution of change or an elevation of a standard.

Which gets us to being an amalgamated advocate in today's America – and another reason why I decided to put this collection of writings together.

As Diary of a Mad, Black PYC talks about – the novelty of Black conservatism in The Obama Era is one that often does not do justice to the dynamic that Black Republicans should play in today's politics. As a Black Republican and conservative, I get that. And, because the dynamic allows for a sacred delineation between one's conservatism and one's Blackness (or at least it would seem), many Black Republicans and conservatives (because, after all, there is a bevy of Black conservatives that will not claim the Republican Party for whatever reason, be it political differences or media/economic expediency) often refuse to claim their Blackness in a strong, public fashion while simultaneously extolling their conservative values and stances. Now, I'm not referring to Black conservatives telling audiences about their hardships growing up. I'm specifically referring to Black Republicans failing to share current experiences with more of Black America while, at the same time, promoting and articulating modern-day conservatism (and even Tea Party activism) with any real sense of consistency and depth. As this trend has continued in several pockets of American political thought, the phenomenon of Black Republicans feeling comfortable to talk to White audiences about their Blackness and talk to Black audiences about their conservatism in various arenas (e.g., speaking to high schools on the South Side of Chicago, then heading up to speak with Tea Party activists in suburbia) does not occur often enough. I know that in many of my speeches and articles, I try my best to exemplify what I am and who I am at all times. It would be disingenuous to hide the struggles that I have engaged as an urban Black male. It would cheat my testimony if I did not portray my beliefs as a Christian conservative on life issues or my sincerity in asking for decorum in debating today's tough issues. It would be haphazard to speak to fiscal conservatives about the runaway issues of spending at the local and state levels (which, of course, eventually find their ways in the halls up on Capitol Hill) if I did not also speak of many of the conditions that contribute to these woes. And, yes, I often get asked about why I feel the need to speak so much about race and why I feel required to identify myself with race – with being Black, with being "African-American", and with being a Black father and husband in today's America.

If I may speak my thoughts freely...

I do so – and, as a result, I felt the need to put this collection together - because we as Americans are nothing but a nation of amalgamated people. We are nothing but a collection of individual melting pots, coming together in the diversity of these United States that blends cultures, races, ethnicities, languages, geographical backgrounds, and life experiences in the greatest experiment – and civic experience – known to mankind. Not being honest enough with the people that I love personally and the nation that I love patriotically to speak on my personal amalgamation of Black, White, Catholic, conservative, Pittsburgh, Davidson, Chicago, father, husband, public figure, public speaker, victim, survivor, warrior, visionary, friend, believer – what good would any words coming out of my mouth be?

When I am at the lectern or at the "notepad", about to articulate what is on my mind, I feel the pressure. I feel the pressure of making sure that those that feel abandoned in society in 2012 have a voice through me. Besides, without people like me speaking up for the folks that I sit beside on the #4 bus or the #6 bus riding through Hyde Park and Woodlawn here on the South Side, will they ever have a voice at all, especially within the annuls of Republican political thought? I feel the pressure of living up to the obligation of representing the good hearts and strong character of thousands of well-natured Tea Party activists that I have met over the years whenever I am confronted with fallacies such as all Tea Party activists are Klan-adoring racists that want to "take back America" through the extermination of Black people or the mass emigration of Spanish-speaking people from the United States. Through my amalgamation in what makes me an American and my advocacy for what makes me love this nation, I feel the obligation –and yes, the pressure – to speak on behalf of poor, working class people that will never have a chance to speak to anchors on CNN or Current TV or Fox News or National Public Radio. I feel the need to make sure that I present my conservative viewpoints in an honorable way that will facilitate liberty AND prosperity for those in most need of both, not those that have the luxury to pontificate the values of those words from a perch above the national crisis at hand today. I feel the responsibility to represent my Penn Hills background when I sit on Capitol Hill just as much as I must articulate the vision that government has (or should have) when I am sitting on a desk in a high school classroom full of teenage parents, former truants, and unfocused schoolboys.

To be direct, I feel like I have no other choice but to share Spoken Thoughts from an Amalgamated Advocate in Today's America because these thoughts, at the very least, are thoughts that express the amalgamated nature that most American leaders and advocates must effectively share if we are going to uplift a greater swath of Americans for a better harvest of our talents and potential for the future. Sometimes, as Black people, we are still too afraid to act on our political conservative beliefs; (granted, 2008 seemed to have changed that, but perhaps not entirely). Sometimes, as conservatives, we are still inclined to forfeit the struggles of improving race relations to progressive leaders, many of whom have not adequately advanced the issues jamming up race relations and disparities in America for years now. Sometimes, as working class Americans, we are too petrified in our poverty or our fears to speak out against the wrongs that we see all around us out of concern for losing the little that we have. Just as well, there are times when we as political insiders refuse to roll back our sleeves and speak, think, and act as humble, servant leaders that would rather give up the shoes on our feet than have someone polish them for us at a shoeshine stand instead.

It takes an amalgamated set of experiences to relate to an increasingly diverse, complex, and troubled America.

It takes an advocate that can engage all of that comfortably, only to think through what must change, speak new realities into formation, and act out of love to make it so for the advancement of the American Dream for more of us.

These are just some of my spoken thoughts in the hope of doing my part to bring about just that. I may be naive to some, but I believe, and as an advocate, belief is both a requirement and the lifeblood in the quest for a better America. I may not be typical or orthodox, but amalgamated people like you and me – people with storybook life tales and the bumps and bruises as proof of our journeys – never fit inside the mold. Our thoughts – both spoken and written – break the mold, just as we break the mold as Americans, be it in politics, civics, or otherwise.

Here's to hoping that my Spoken Thoughts challenge you to think, inspire you to speak, and stay with you as you act – all for the sake of a better future for us all.

SPEECHES: The Spoken Thoughts

Lenny McAllister: Atlanta Tea Party 1-year anniversary
2010 Feb 27 ("**Mandating American Exceptionalism**")

Good afternoon, Atlanta Tea Party Patriots!

Congratulations on your one-year anniversary, and kudos on your good work over the course of your first year!

It is because of your daily dedication over the past year that a movement - started by a small group of grassroots Americans - showed a large group of astro-turf politicians that the only change that we can believe in for America is a change back to what America is supposed to be for us all: the land of opportunity, a nation of personal freedom, and a country protecting our collective pursuit of happiness.

I congratulate you for reminding America over the past year that it is truly un-American to place an unconstitutional mandate for purchasing government-guided health care around the necks of each and every American. In 2009, we rallied against those that want to give us health care mandates. In 2010, we rally to bring about a new collection of our own mandates – calls to action that will call to task those in Washington that view their time in Congress as their luxurious chance to limit freedom, not a calling to lead America to limitless prosperity **through** freedom.

President Obama and his supporters on Capitol Hill may believe in the health care mandates from 2009, but we are here today to ensure them that we believe in the electoral mandates of November 2010 – and if the images of this health care debate do not change over the next few weeks, the faces in Congress **will** change within the next few months.

I thank you, Tea Party Patriots, for doing the impossible – waking up the masses of the apathetic, uninspired, and unengaged within our nation and re-energizing them within the civic and political fabric that binds us together as a common people. Not long ago, Americans used to take the unique beauty of this country for granted, but now everyday citizens are following the steps of our government to make sure that our government follows the steps listed in our Constitution. And we are assured – everyday Americans are now ready to act in force when the representative government refuses to act in kind.

That is because of tea party people like you here today, because sometimes, you just can't wake a person up from a deep sleep, even with dousing a bucket of cold water on 'em. However, this party of people has proven over the past year that you can wake a nation up – with just a splash of TEA.

We come here today to the State Capitol as patriots to mark a historic anniversary in Atlanta at a time when the nation – the honor of our past and our obligation to the future – calls us to be historic. We gather together as children born from impossible paths to fight for the possibility of a better American journey. We voice our concerns as a community of believers that reject what is popular for what is right and we reject what some call impossible because we know that in America – anything of the ultimate good from a loving God is possible. We live as witnesses of perpetual constitutional victory – where a descendant of Africans can stand in an area where slaves were once sold to say to my fellow Americans that we must know our facts in the midst of opposition, respect our ideological enemies in the midst of debate, and love our nation in the midst of internal tension more than we fear being labeled as a group of the uninformed, a movement of hatred, and believers in the impossible dream.

For we know that this is a lie if we remain focused on our goals as a movement.

Our willingness to be informed citizens must make us the most powerful citizenry in the world. Our dedicated love of God, family, and country must lift us above perceived hatred of others. Our Constitution will crush the impossible dream through the resources of free markets, civic equality, and a representative government by the people to give us a better civic revelation - the American Dream.

You did the impossible over the past year when many said that conservatism was dead. Now, we must be aware that it is still time for us to make possible the conservative changes that America needs today.

Many will say to you that we do not have the numbers or the willpower to change this current direction of big government despite our best efforts... regardless of the results in Virginia, New Jersey, and Massachusetts. They will say to you that we do not have enough momentum to restore the time-honored constitutionality that made America the beacon of the world...regardless of the retirements of several legislators that bet on the power of popular trends and political machines over the power of the American people – **and lost.** They will point you to history and tell you that American change has always involved accepting the status quo, feel-good solutions from big government and liberalism that were offered to us at the time.

I say to you today: that, too, is a lie.

We reject big government as the best solution. If we took the big government perspective in colonial America, the enormity of the British Empire – the Empire that never had the sun set on it - would have never lost to upstart patriots in the American Revolutionary War.

We reject the stance of status quo. If we decided to follow the status quo voiced in America in the 1930s by ignoring global evil, we would have never courageously overcome the wickedness of the Third Reich that led in acts of pre-emptive murder in Europe, Asia, and in Pearl Harbor.

We reject the suggestion that we lack what it takes. If we decided that we did not have enough numbers, resources, or momentum to follow our Constitution in the 1950s, we would have never overcome adversity together with Dr. Martin Luther King, Jr. and other brave Americans in pursuing Dr. King's Dream in the 1960s and beyond.

And we reject the notion that America welcomes a socialist way of solving problems. If we decided to accept socialism as a common denominator for us in the world, we would have never watched President Reagan ask Mikhail Gorbachev to tear down the Wall of communism – and then watch it fall in Berlin years later.

We stand today because others stood victorious when the times called for them to take a stand.

We are witnesses to history today because those before us were willing to be historic in the face of threats against domestic and international freedom. We are a nation of fighters, kindred of valor, and a whirlwind of persistence. We are a nation that is one-of-a-kind, not one that kindly asks to be one just like everybody else. We don't desire for the European model of living – we aspire to best it. We are the nation with a history rich in making new and better possibilities for Americans and those throughout the world regularly…out of the very things that others say to us are impossibilities – but that we refuse to accept as impossible.

That includes a new America without its current big government approach and spending.

That includes health care reform without the current partisan slant to it and government mandate in it.

That includes more tax revenue without higher tax rates because more Americans are working while less Americans are unemployed, underemployed, and suffering.

So, as witnesses **to** history and patriots *for* tomorrow, we come together today to ask the president and his friends on Capitol Hill- **this**:

if we were unwilling to tolerate tyranny from Great Britain, unwilling to overlook wickedness from the Third Reich, unwilling to be hypocritical with civil rights in the 20th century, and unwilling to compromise freedom with communism, what makes you think that we will merely accept the tyrannical mandates coming out of Washington today, complete with an economic wickedness that is hell-bent on destroying dreams with job-killing legislation, and promoting socialistic endeavors and calling it social equality?

I say to you today, fellow patriots: we will not. We will not sit still for a health care mandate this spring, especially as we know that there is an election full of mandates that we will empower America with through our votes in the fall.

Patriots, we stand today because others stood victorious when the times called for them to take a stand, just as the time beckons us now to take a stand – with love, with respect, and with honor – all with American history on our side.

And I say that with this in mind. I view the president with respect as an American. I stand with the commander-in-chief in support when others in the world look to disrespect or threaten America. But I say with conviction that I passionately disagree with the president because he – and others – do not get that the American people do not want a health care mandate that the Constitutional spirit of America mandates against.

After your work in the past year, the White House eventually determined that jobs should be the #1 priority in 2010 instead of health care, basically saying that the White House and majority leadership on Capitol Hill finally get it about jobs – of course, after listening to people like you during the health care debate last summer.

Well, I'm here to say that I'm glad that the President, the Speaker of the House, and the Senate Majority Leader get that jobs are #1, but it is tragic that they waited to get it now while too many Americans got it month after month under their watch as communities of Americans were stripped of their ability to provide for their families as jobs atrophied while government spending grew exponentially.

But that is not all of what we got from the mandate-driving paradigm of leadership in Washington.

From this paradigm of leadership, we received a paradox in messaging.

As we stand here at the end of Black History Month 2010, what we got in 2009 was a presidential speech to the NAACP about the value of education for disadvantaged Black students, only to see the White House cut funding to Republican-initiated programs for these same students – all while sending money to commit murder on the unborn overseas via a presidential executive order while too many American children remained undeveloped academically here at home.

Recently, we saw a presidential speech promoting the journey of the downtrodden in America towards prosperity, only to see the White House promote budgets and proposals that substantially kill better employment opportunities, better educational opportunities, and better business ownership opportunities while substantially increasing entitlement benefits simultaneously.

Mr. President, I ask humbly, respectfully, and passionately: when will your colleagues finally accept that President Lyndon Johnson's Great Society has not has a great positive effect on America?

When will you and your colleagues accept that welfare does not lead to accumulating wealth – jobs do.

When will you and your colleagues accept that government-mandated health care will never make Americans as healthy as having a healthy dose of jobs available for them will do?

Jobs stimulate family stability, prosperity, and wealth. These factors create access to better education. Better educated people are better equipped to utilize the best health care quality in the world – without government having to pay for it, fix it, or do it for them. Better educated people are better prepared to respect, defend, and enjoy liberty and equality in the 21st century –

without government having to do it for us.

The healthy without jobs become the downtrodden in our streets. The downtrodden in our streets fill our hospital beds without insurance. The government's hand in health care will never return a lost home, but the free market's creation of more jobs and health care competition can ward off future misfortunes.

To our fellow Americans that are liberal, we say today: THAT is why we must focus on jobs first, not government-guided health care. That is why American free-market innovation and competition must be trusted with jobs and with health care as they were with technology - **more** than we trust modeling ourselves after questionable health care systems that overly tax our global neighbors throughout the world. While the president and the liberals in Congress attempt to catch up to Europe in the long-term pursuit of big government direction and government-run health care, I say that it is well beyond time for the president and Congress to catch up to the American people and focus on solutions that will create jobs first , not more government…in a nation full of willing workers, not welfare seekers…for a collection of Americans willing to dream to be historic, not watch the American Dream become history.

The American Dream is about choices that defend liberty and life. Just the same the Tea Party Movement – from defending against government's overreach in the health care field or the pointless spending that has mostly succeeded at stimulating a "jobless recovery"- it is about defending liberty and life. And just the same, Tea Party Patriots have a love of country and are called to love, respect, and lead their fellow Americans because of their choice to promote liberty and life.

Our pursuit of happiness on this 1-year anniversary in Atlanta must always include a commitment to defending liberty and life. The pursuit of happiness is a choice to be historic and the obligation to ensure that future Americans have the option to do the same. Our celebration of the movement today must entail an oath to explaining our history and our future with facts and honor – not emotionalism or disrespect. We must uphold a mandate amongst ourselves that uplifts the highest level of ethics and Americanism so that demeanor is beyond reproach and our arguments are the focus of the day.

And why is this important?

For in an age where America has grown fat on government…at a time when America is re-awaking to reclaim its future…and as we see our nation looking for true direction…we must remember that history is on our side and be determined to rightfully be historic.

America is the land where the impossible for the sake of what is right **is always possible**, thanks to the power of the people and the mandate for liberty and life that is our Constitution.

President Obama, Speaker Pelosi, and Majority Leader Reid - we always remember that the Constitution is one mandate that will never fail us.

And for those that may forget that fact? They will soon remember once again…as soon as this party of patriots gives them another splash of tea.

Thank you for this opportunity to speak to you today. God Bless you all and God Bless the United States of America.

Chairman Bond, thank you for the invitation to speak today. Along with Assistant Treasurer Jesse Turner, Jr., you have dedicated yourselves for decades to bringing about diversity and equality. At this critical time in American history, it is important for others to see that we can embrace the diversity within Black America so that together, we can fix the problems plaguing Black America. Thank you for understanding this.

Vice Chairman Brock and President Jealous, I thank you for your willingness to seek out advocates in all circles. Although our politics may be different, our love for community is not. Just as I represent a change for the Republican Party, you represent a new wave of young leaders that are committed to raising the bar even higher. Thank you for embracing this call.

The leadership of the NAACP Board of Directors is just one example of the wealth of insight and experiences we share within our communities. We must use all these resources of talent to address the issues affecting us collectively as a people and as a nation. It will take a network of caring leaders to bridge African-Americans over the lingering effects of our past to the promise of our future. The NAACP Board of Directors is one important cog of that network. I thank the Board for their passion and dedication to serving the disadvantaged among us.

As a proud member of the Prince George's County Chapter of the NAACP during my tenure as Lieutenant Governor of Maryland, I am honored to be here today. Before I continue, I extend a thank you on behalf of two of my staff members: Angela Sailor and Paris Dennard of the Coalitions Department. They are pleased to be Town Hall participants at the 2009 NAACP Leadership 500 Summit.

Collectively, our RNC team understands that relationships between us at the RNC and members throughout the NAACP network have been positive and effective. We must continue the work together if we are to continue building The Dream for us all.

On the heels of America's celebration of her 233rd birthday comes the centennial convention of this proud organization.

It is only fitting that the Party of Lincoln be part of this centennial. It is ironic, and perhaps even symbolic, that its chairman be an African-American at this time.

For, on February 12, 1909 – the 100th birthday of President Abraham Lincoln - the NAACP was born. This organization was created 9 years to the day after the Negro National Anthem was  written as part of a celebration of Lincoln's Birthday. Its founders were a group of brave visionaries from varying backgrounds. It included those that were Republicans. Perhaps the most prominent African-American Republican of the group was James Weldon Johnson, the co-author of "Lift Ev'ry Voice and Sing."

Before becoming the first African-American to lead the NAACP in 1920, Johnson was a leader in the Republican Party. He served as treasurer of the Colored Republican Club in 1904 before becoming its president one year later. By1906 Johnson had become a US Consul in Venezuela. In 1909, he transferred to become a US Consul in Nicaragua. Both posts were bestowed upon Johnson by Republican presidents.

Johnson went on to serve the NAACP from 1914 through 1930, serving the last 10 years in leadership. He used a balance of social activism and political moxie to be a leader that ushered in progress for America. He is a precursor to modern times. His example shows us that Republican values and social progress can effectively make sense for Black America.

Another prominent Republican from our proud, collective history is Dr. Channing H. Tobias. As a lifelong Republican that pursued civil rights, Dr. Tobias influenced religious and secular organizations to spread the message of cooperation between all Americans, regardless of race, creed, and other affiliations. In 1923, Dr. Tobias was appointed Senior Secretary in the Department of Interracial Services within the Colored Work Department of the YMCA, where he served for over 2 decades.

From that post, Dr. Tobias prospered as a respected international speaker on interracial affairs. He served on numerous leadership boards, including the Commission on the Church and Minority Groups of the Federal Council of Churches. He was a member of the board of trustees for Howard University, Hampton Institute, and the NAACP.

Just a look at these two historical examples provides some insight into why the NAACP has an important tie to the Party of Lincoln. It is a bond that we must not undervalue or under-utilize if we are to reverse trends of under-performance within our communities today.

Not surprisingly, the GOP was formed to reverse negative trends.

As a moral contrast to the Democrats' pro-slavery agenda, abolitionists founded the Republican Party on March 20, 1854. The Republican National Committee met for the first time in 1856. The first Republican National Convention was held later that year. By 1860, Abraham Lincoln won the White House and Republicans won majorities in both houses of Congress. In addition, the governors of every northern state in America were Republicans. This was possible because the Republican Party espouses the belief that our nation, conceived in personal liberty and dedicated to equality for all, must live up to its founding principles. Republican successes in 1860 sharply opposed the direction Southern Democrats heeded at that time.

The rest, they say, is history.

The Republican Party quickly became known as the Party of Lincoln because of the president's leadership to unify the nation and eliminate the institution of slavery. The Emancipation Proclamation remains one of the most significant documents in American history. Our annual Juneteenth Celebration is a joyous remembrance of Union soldiers reaching the slaves of Galveston, Texas to inform them of Lincoln's freeing words.

However, Lincoln sought to do more than just free slaves. The president sought freedom *for* the slaves. He understood that true freedom comes from the right of self-determination by way of a representative government. Perhaps that is why in his last public address at the White House, President Lincoln expressed his support for Black suffrage.

His assailant, John Wilkes Booth, was on hand for Lincoln's remarks. Three days later, he killed The Great Emancipator.

But as we know from the story of Joseph in the Old Testament and the life of Dr. Martin Luther King, Jr. –

You can attack the Dreamer, but you cannot destroy the Dream.

Such was the case of the Republican vision for America after Lincoln.

For the next one hundred years, Republicans stood against those that sought to destroy both dreamers and their dreams. They fought in the annuals of governments and with the conscience of our nation to advance equality for all Americans. In fact, the diversity we enjoy today stems from the adversity they overcame.

A Republican-led Congress passed the 13th Amendment to outlaw slavery.

Republicans passed a Civil Rights Act in 1866 recognizing blacks as U.S. citizens.

Republicans continued their march for equality, proposing the 14th Amendment, which became part of the Constitution in 1868.

Republicans also led the fight for women's rights. Women's suffragists Susan B. Anthony and NAACP co-founders Ida B. Wells and Mary Terrell all displayed loyalty to the Republican Party due to our historic commitment to equality.

Senator Aaron Sargent, a Republican from California, wrote the women's suffrage amendment. Unfortunately, it was delayed from being passed into law for 40 years. It took a time when Republicans had control of both houses of Congress before women's voting rights could be secured by law.

The age of women's suffrage brought about a new era of women's representation in government. The first woman elected to the U.S. House of Representatives was Republican Jeannette Rankin of Montana. The first woman mayor in America, Republican Bertha Landes, was elected in 1926.

More generations of women civic leaders came afterwards, from Governors Jodi Rell of Connecticut and Jan Brewer of Arizona to US Senators Lisa Murkowski of Alaska and Kay Bailey Hutchinson of Texas.

Of course, I would be remiss if I did not mention former Secretary of State Condoleezza Rice, the second consecutive African-American Republican to serve as secretary of state this decade.

Secretaries of State Rice and Powell do not represent all of the African-American Republican political leaders that we share in our common history. In fact, every African-American member of Congress until 1935 was a Republican.

Among these Republican pioneers was South Carolina's Joseph Rainey, the first Black member of the House of Representatives. Republican Hiram Revels of Mississippi entered the Halls of Congress with Rainey as the first Black United States Senator. In 1872, Republican Pinckney Pinchback of Louisiana became the nation's first African-American Governor, an accomplishment only matched by the Democrats over 100 years later.

From Republican Congressmen Oscar Stanton de Priest of Illinois and JC Watts of Oklahoma to Senator Edward Brooke of Massachusetts, we have stood proudly for diversity: in government as African-Americans and as Republicans in modern-day Black America.

For 100 years, Republicans stood up for what was right even when it was wrongly opposed.

Starting in 1875, Republicans enacted laws to expand federally-protected rights to include equal access to all public accommodations. The Supreme Court struck down their efforts eight years later, only to have these efforts resurface as a critical foundation for the 1964 Civil Rights Act down the road.

America remembered that you can attack the Dreamer, but you cannot destroy the Dream.

Republican President Teddy Roosevelt spoke out several times on the horrors of lynching. He wrote a direct plea to the governor of Indiana, a state known at the time as a bastion of the Klan.

He said,

> "All thoughtful men...must feel the gravest alarm over the growth of lynching in this country, and especially over the peculiarly hideous forms so often taken by mob violence when colored men are the victims..."

Under Presidents Roosevelt and Taft in 1909, legislators began introducing more than 200 bills in Congress to make lynching a federal crime, but they failed to pass, primarily due to Democratic opposition in Washington.

When the Ku Klux Klan rose to prominence in the 1920s, Republican Presidents Warren Harding and Calvin Coolidge denounced KKK violence by supporting new federal anti-lynching legislation. This law passed in the Republican House but, again, repeatedly died in the Democrat-controlled Senate.

Discouraged but not demoralized, Republican legislators and Republican activists such as NAACP matriarch Ida B. Wells fought on until the occurrences of lynching ceased, becoming our common scar from a painful past.

After years of opposition to civil rights legislation by the Democratic Party, the landmark Civil Rights Act became American law. This happened after Republicans triumphed over a Democratic filibuster to block the bill. Over 80% of Republicans voted for the Civil Rights Act, carrying the act by a far greater percentage than the Democrats, completing a legislative path taken decades earlier.

Again, you can attack the Dreamer, but you cannot destroy the Dream.

Now, today, we fairly ask: if you can attack dreamers of equality and freedom but you cannot destroy their dreams of a better America, then what caused the divide between the Party of Lincoln and proud African-Americans post-slavery?

We know that throughout Reconstruction, African-Americans and Republicans intermingled as patriots with common agendas, perspectives, and identities to promote civil rights. Many African-Americans stayed Republican, enduring property threats to their homes and physical threats at the polls before being disenfranchised.

The Great Depression was a time when all Americans were looking for help during a dark hour in America. The programs offered by FDR served as the re-introduction of the Democratic Party to African-Americans that were afforded the ability to vote. These social programs sought to put Americans back to work and keep Americans in their homes. Sadly, Roosevelt's vision of a booming American economy because of big government was never realized. It was only achieved because of the boom of violence that rocked the world – an epic time later known as World War II.

Over the past several decades, the Republican Party has done a poor job of reflecting its proud history. My party's former use of the "Southern Strategy" has been denounced as a tactic that exploited the wounds of American racism to gain advantages in elections. Coupled with some insensitive and repugnant statements and behaviors by a minority of high-profile conservatives, a portion of the recent history of the Republican Party has overcast the high-minded direction that my party has taken since its inception.

It is unfortunate and it is intolerable.

However, just as I require of my team at the RNC, so I ask of you today:
We must not allow the missteps of a few to overlook the great strides that the Party of Lincoln and Black America have made together to improve this great nation.

We must not overlook the benefits of the bond between the time-tested principles of the Republican Party and the founding ideals of the NAACP. As well, we should not glaze over the results that Black America that experienced since our political migration began some decades ago.

Exactly where has our political migration taken us over the past 5 decades?

On his campaign to the White House, then-Senator John F. Kennedy addressed the NAACP on July 10, 1960. He laid out a promise of what his leadership would bring, leadership that has become the envy of many politicians leading our towns, cities, and states over the past 5 decades.

In dealing with discrimination, he said that we should:

"Let us trust no one who offers slick and easy answers - for the only final answer will come from the work of thousands of individual answers, large and small, in the Congress, the courts and the White House, in states and cities all over America, in the actions of brave and wise public servants, and in the reactions of determined private citizens…"

Yet, in our recent past, we have collectively chosen a path that trusts government more and diminishes our role as private citizens in the work to eliminate discrimination in all its forms. This path contravenes the examples set by this organization and Black America historically, examples co-authored with Republicans, including Black Republicans.

He said in dealing with employment and education:

"What we are seeking, after all, is really very simple…the right of every man to work as he wants to work, to be educated as every human being deserves to be educated…"

Yet, as we look at the recent trends within Black America regarding our showing in employment status and in the classroom, we find a very disturbing pattern of low expectations and performances. Further disturbing is that studies comparing African-American academic barometers and other significant social factors to other Americans from around the time of Kennedy's speech mirror what we find in 2009 in Black America. All this we find during the growth of bureaucracy in our local and state governments since the 1960s, a period when we betrayed our historic example of trust in self with expensive investments in programs.

Our return on investment has been negligible.

Then-Senator Kennedy also noted that African-Americans should also enjoy:

> "The right of all people to be free from the tensions and terrors and burdens of war, its preparation and its consequences."

But after years of political control by mostly one party within the vast majority of our urban centers throughout America, we are now regularly faced with those tensions, terrors, and burdens of war. We are faced with them as we walk to the neighborhood store. Our children are faced with them as they walk to school each day. We are losing our loved ones and our future to the horrific tensions and terrors and burdens of war that we see in our streets. Our Baghdad often is Baltimore. Our combat zone is too often Chicago.

In looking back at our collective history, I fear that our lack of policy knowledge and preparation has led to unanticipated and unprecedented consequences: growth of American government and bureaucracy that paralleled violence in our streets and the destruction of our families in Black America.

Just as we as African-Americans decided to vote on the side of history in 1960, many of us voted to be on the side of history again in 2008.

However, as we look at the continued conditions of the American people and of Black America particularly, it is time to us to re-examine our past examples of progress and consider getting on the right side of history starting now. Looking over our mutual history of freedom and of civil rights, it is clear: the Republican Party and the NAACP share the history, principles, and directives that benefit Black America. They must be embraced again if we are to be successful in addressing the challenges facing us today. We must rehabilitate and reinvigorate the bond that we share.

How do we do this? We pursue policies that advance the Dream: namely, equal employment opportunities.

For Republican President Richard Nixon, rehabilitating this bond meant supporting anti-discrimination laws with substance by increasing the civil rights enforcement budget 8-fold with over $600 million in allocated resources by the end of his first term.

He looked to model the successes of Black Wall Street and other entrepreneurial successes that advanced Black people. He knew that increasing jobs and innovation would do reinvigorate Black America more than growing government ever could. That is why the president signed an executive order establishing the Office of Minority Business Enterprise, now renamed the Minority Business Development Agency.

In the first two years of his administration, federal purchases from minority firms increased more than 1,000%. Small Business Administration lending to minority enterprises grew over 400% under this leadership, from $41.3 million in fiscal year 1968 to $195 million in fiscal year 1971.

How do we continue to rehabilitate and reinvigorate the bond we share? We pursue policies that advance another important facet of the Dream: namely, equality in education.

That is why President Ronald Reagan established Executive Order 12320 within his first year in office. With the White House Initiative on Historically Black Colleges and Universities, the president directed the Secretary of Education to develop of a federal program designed to increase participation by historically Black colleges and universities in federally-sponsored programs.

Republican leadership looked to strengthen Black employment and Black entrepreneurship simultaneously. With the support of

Executive Order 12320 and the Reagan tax cuts, millions of African-Americans went on to become college graduates, businesses owners, and homeowners.

The president shared a common understanding with us: that employment of parents fosters sound education for children, and that the two - together - drive our economy.

With African-Americans building more for their lives by keeping more of their hard-earned money, they started building for themselves the American Dream. Once again, it was proof that you can attack the dreamers, but you cannot destroy the Dream.

During President Reagan's last 7 years in office, Black unemployment was cut by roughly 50% while White unemployment dropped by only 4%.

During the Reagan Era, the average household income for African-Americans went up by over 80%, outpacing White household income increases throughout the decade of the 1980s.

Black-owned businesses increased from 308,000 in 1982 to 424,000 in 1987 - a 38% rise - with receipts by Black-owned firms doubling to $19.8 billion over the same period of time.

President George H. W. Bush continued President Reagan's commitment to Historically Black Colleges and Universities. In his first year of office, he signed Executive Order 12677 to create a Presidential Advisory Board to advise the Secretary of Education in methods strengthening these valued institutions.

And the much-maligned President George W. Bush? Through 2009, he was the president that promoted the most diversity in a presidential administration in history.

He appointed the first two African-American Secretaries of State in American history.

His record levels of diversity within the administration continued, with several key posts within his administration filled with people of color.

His concern for humanity stretched across the ocean. President Bush met with 25 African heads of state within his first 2 years in office. He tripled humanitarian aid to Africa to nearly $9 billion. His many acts to improve conditions of Africans are well-known to those in the Motherland.

Some historical bonds are just too important to break or ignore.

Through their actions, recent Republican presidents understood what we understand here today. They enacted what our NAACP founders and predecessors knew: that economic opportunities and educational improvements are intertwined, and those two, working together, usher out poverty and ring in equality.

With this in mind, it makes sense that Republican principles are common ideals shared with the NAACP to benefit Black America.

As well, it makes sense for us to ask the question, "Where do we go – working together - from here?"

President Ben Jealous noted in a recent editorial on CNN that "...the election of President Obama is the result of a decades-long fight for political inclusion." For the sake of improving America, I respectfully challenge us today to continue the fight for something more.

Our American inclusion in politics and society must be more than 90% of us voting for one political party exclusively while

15% of us are unemployed, as reported as of May of this year. Our American inclusion in the cities and towns of America must be more than incorporating the same failed approaches to urban issues, only to encounter the same tragic results repeatedly, as we have for decades now.

As a people, we must stop fighting the Struggle with one political arm tied behind our backs as we will need all of our strength to take hold of the issues before us and grasp the promise our ancestors bequeathed us.

As a party, Republicans must articulate the benefits of our policies and display why these policies will benefit Black America.

As a people, we must judge people by the content of their character in the political realm. We must examine the policies of a politician and not just the persona of a man. We must learn from our past and examine our present to find the best solutions for our future.

As a party, Republicans must be good ambassadors of our principles. We must show the commonalities that we share with minorities, from our shared history of courageously changing America for the better to our common insistence that God must be a part of the daily American Way of Life.

Claiming Republican history with Black America must no longer be a cop-out by my party in order to get minority votes in November. Under my leadership, it will stop being that cop-out and it will become a continuation of the monumental progress that the NAACP and Republicans have made together since the inception of this organization.

It is important for Republicans to say that we are sorry for not engaging minorities appropriately, but it is more important for

Republicans to *show* that we are sorry through initiating efforts that display our willingness to partner with Black America. That is currently happening under my leadership and I pledge to you that it will continue.

As well, it is important for Black America to hear these apologies from the Republican Party, but it is more important for Black America to remove the typecasting and other barriers that prevent us from continuing the historical partnership that brought America so much progress. I come to the NAACP today just as I went to the State of Black Union in February, extending the hand of the GOP for a new era of partnership. I hope that it is time that we join hands and join forces and together, we continue building The Dream.

For as a people, we must debate political and social solutions with open minds, loving hearts, and common goals, goals that further the promise of The Dream.

As a collection of leaders, we must take on attacks of rhetoric with honest debate. We must take on attacks of pain and prejudice with truth and tenacity. We must take on attacks of ignorance that divide us with vision and knowledge that educate us and unite us.

We can do these things from both sides of the political aisle in Black America. Although some in the recent past have tarnished the bonds that tie us together, they can never completely destroy the bond Republicans, the NAACP, and Black America share. It is a bond of freedom. It is a bond of equality. It is a bond of progress. It is a bond that fosters The Dream.

And as we see over the 100 years of the NAACP, they may attack us, the dreamers, but if we work together, they will never be able to destroy The Dream.

Thank you for this opportunity. God Bless you all and God Bless the United States of America.

*Lenny McAllister: MLK Day Celebration in Ocala, FL (2010 January 18 ("**MLK Day, Furthering The Dream of Yesterday, and Waking Up for a Better Future**"))*

People may wonder why it was important to me to come with prepared words to address you today. Many of you may state – and rightfully so- that we gather today to honor the accomplishments of Dr. Martin Luther King Jr., a man that was moved by the Spirit to move a nation towards a better way of life. And you would be right – Dr. King was a man that used his connection to the Holy Spirit to dare to have The Dream. At the same time, my fellow Americans, he also had action items, and without action items – along with a network of leaders and fellow dreamers – we would not have a MLK Day each year and chances are that we would not have the expression of civil rights that we enjoy today. Therefore, I come to you with action items to further Dr. King's dream and ask that we honor the man and his memory with more than just talk of dreams.

President Lincoln used a speech that started "4 score and 7 years ago" in order to call his beleaguered countrymen to continue their march towards unity of our nation during its most trying hour. Now, here we come today, 2 score and 7 years past the date of Dr. King's "I Have a Dream" speech, speaking up in order to call our beleaguered communities to act so that we can continue our march towards equal rights as Americans, equal opportunities as contributors to our nation, and equal kindred in the brotherhood of prosperity and visionary leadership of this great land.

King's efforts and sacrifices came those scores of years ago, but our time to continue his accomplishments and dream is right now. It is before us here in the Sunshine State. It is in our hands in each state of Lincoln's Union.

Without the sustained march towards realizing the fullest details of King's Dream, we are hampered in our march towards bettering our fellow man. Although we are capable and encouraged to help the victims in Haiti through the epic tragedy they are incurring, we are limited in restoring their communities if we lag behind in our societal, educational, and economic potential here in America. Although it is best to encourage and mentor our schoolchildren today with the pursuits of their youth, we are limited in leading our children into a prosperous future if we impede our discipline, communicative channels, and networking relationships that could make the difference in their lives with limiting stereotypes, outdated misunderstandings, and esteem for others and ourselves. Although we are free from slavery, Jim Crow, and many glass ceilings from the American past, we are boxed into probabilities of failure and disappointment if we are not willing to actively work towards being freer than the previous generation, healthier than we were just a year ago, and better than we were just yesterday.

Dr. King worked aside a network of leaders and everyday Americans. He came at a time when America needed a dream – a new vision for what the United States could be once united past the impediments of racism and self-limitations. He came with a Dream that talked about his children being equal but spoke to America about opening up its potential to becoming a superpower of wealth, might, and ethical esteem throughout the world by shedding its racism of the past and embracing the moment to be historic.

President Lincoln had Americans such as Frederick Douglass to push him to greater heights as the Great Emancipator, just as Dr. King had Freedom Fighters and others that believed in the push for Civil Rights.

Lincoln noted change "4 score and 7 years ago" during his time in Gettysburg to reunite America. King told us 2 score and 7 years ago that he had a dream for a better time for America.

Today, I say that it is time to even the scores throughout America.

It is time for us to even the scores of our schoolchildren with others as they have fallen behind other American children in the classroom. It is time to demand better facilities, better teachers, and better school options with our tax money. A better educated child will be a more active citizen in our communities and a source of pride for Black America as an adult.

It is time for us to even the scores in the job market, as African-Americans are still more likely to be last-hired and first-fired. It is time to even the playing field, one that today sees that Black men are twice as likely to be unemployed with college degrees as other American men with similar levels of education. It is time to ensure that equality is not just a slogan from the past, but it is an umbrella promise for the future for all Americans.

It is time for us to even the scores and lessen the rate of disease, disillusionment, and even death at our own hands. It is time to even the scores within the fields of health care, crime, and chivalry once again with other Americans. It is time for us to stop killing each other with our diets. It is time for us to stop killing each other with weapons. It is time to stop killing each other's esteem with disrespect for our women. It is time for Black pride to rise up through teaching Black love, Black self-respect, Black family unity, and Black chivalry and stop speaking solely with a tone of blaming others, looking outside our communities for solutions, and embracing sub-standard realities for our children and grandchildren. King led the disadvantaged towards equality with self-empowerment. We must do the same today.

Dr. King spoke of a Dream for all of America, but he knew that he would take action within Black America for this dream to become reality. Therefore, if we are to take one thing from this MLK Day, I ask that it be this:

If Dr. King dared us to collectively Dream along with him, we must now be called to collectively wake up to honor him.

Wake up, brothers and sisters, and act towards better educational opportunities for our children immediately. Do not allow the continuing failure of the school system in our communities to continue to be the box that limits our children's futures. The status quo of educational poverty must be replaced with a quid pro quo system that rewards educational freedom for our children and nothing else, not political allegiances or backroom deals that cut us out. Be involved as volunteers, as mentors, and as civic activists so that our children receive an education, not just schooling.

Wake up, brothers and sisters, and act towards better quality of life within Black America. Regardless of the health care fight in Washington, if we are unwilling to stop the violence against our bodies with our diets, with our physical confrontations, and with our inactivity, we will always stay behind the health care curve. Wake up to live lest we continue to die prematurely in our sleep. The time is now to change our daily habits so that we change our daily experiences.

Wake up, brothers and sisters, and act towards health care justice for Black America, making sure that we are not the most murdered in the womb and the fastest to lay in the tomb.

Wake up, brothers and sisters, and act towards embracing economic opportunities, equality, and prosperity in America. Embrace Americanism – economically, socially, and historically – with tenacity and insight. This is your nation, too – fully. The red represents our ancestors' sacrifice. The blue represents the depth of talent that we can contribute to America's improvement. The white represents the brightness of our future – together - should we remain engaged in upholding America - together.

There was a time for Dr. King to be historic and Dream. It is now our time to be historic and wake up into action.

If you have not contributed or volunteered to improve our communities, do so now. If you already do contribute, thank you – for now, it is time for us to do more. We must be involved in educational changes, economic changes, and personal changes daily if we are going to wake up from crisis and return to the highest pursuit of Dr. King's Dream.

As I have written in my book, America will only be all that we can be with smaller government along with bigger people. That applies so much more to Black America and the crisis we face today in our communities.

It was a time to dream. Now, it is time to wake up and DO!

Dr. Martin Luther King, Jr. was one of those bigger people when he gave us a Dream to chase after.

Now, we must be those bigger people by waking up into action so that the American Dream – along with Dr. King's Dream – can become a greater reality for us all.

Thank you very much for your time. Thank you, Dr. King, for your love. And thank you all for what you do to improve our communities, save our children, and strengthen our nation. God

Bless you all and God Bless the United States of America.

Lenny McAllister: Ocala Tea Party
2010 January 18 ("**Martin Luther King Was a Tea Party Patriot**")

Good afternoon, Tea Party Patriots.

Thank you for the invitation to address you this afternoon. In a region that is part of the Sunshine State, it is refreshing to see the sunshine reflecting off of your faces today. It is a clear sign that more Americans are becoming engaged with the political processes of their communities and less likely to tolerate a government that has gone on far too long without a true sense of accountability to the Constitution of the United States, the memory of our founding fathers, and the will of a representative republic constituted by one simple phrase: We, The People.

Today, we gather here to protest the direction of government on a day where the nation commemorates the successes of one of its greatest protestors – Dr. Martin Luther King, Jr. Like you, Dr. King saw the need for a change in how our society and government worked in his day, just as we do now. Like you, Dr. King did not wait for others to make a difference in the world – he believed in the power of people over the power of government. Like you, Dr. King saw the vision of a better America coming through  the application of our unique constitution, one that guarantees the enjoyment of inalienable rights from God alone, not through false promises through expansive government that taxes us plenty to give us little. Dr. King knew that holding America to its credos as listed in our Constitution was the way to ensure equality. Just the same, we stand here today knowing that holding our current elected officials to the tenets of representative government is the way to scale back the waywardness in spending and backroom deals that we have seen in Washington, allowing us to regain the effectiveness of our collective voice in government.

In his time, Dr. King stepped outside of societal norms to change the way society operated. That is how he led the Civil Rights Movement.

In our time – right here, right now – we must step outside of politics as normal in order to change the way our government works. That is how we will lead our nation back on track and ensure that America will be a world leader for generations to come.

Dr. King led a movement of people that reclaimed the American Dream 50 years ago. You – the people of the Tea Party movement – are the current leaders that will help reclaim the American Dream for the next 50 years. King fought the good fight against government for American equality for us. Today, we fight the good fight against government for American prosperity for all.

Because of the King example that you are following, if someone comes to you and says that it was inappropriate to have a tea party today or that it was not in line with the message of Dr. Martin Luther King to protest government today, I implore you to remind them with respect that Dr. King rallied against government that restricted personal liberties, just as you are doing today. Remind them that Dr. King marched against laws that contradicted the Constitution, just as you are doing today. Remind them that Dr. King was also called a rabble-rouser, a trouble maker, and a radical without a cause, just as you are called today.

Those that think that you dishonor the memory of Dr. King by speaking out against the continuation of the abomination in Washington on MLK Day obviously do not see one simple fact: that Martin Luther King was a 20th century Tea Party Patriot. Yes, he was – from protesting for a reality that was needed in America before others joined the fight to believing that the Constitution was a time-honored document to be followed by government, not ignored by contemporary politicians chasing partisan glory, big-money contributions, or political philosophies.

And as a Tea Party Patriot, Dr. King would encourage you to protest your government until your government fulfills the obligations enumerated in the founding laws of the land.

He would tell us something that we already know: change will come, but positive, American change will not come from free-spending politicians or big-government program. It will never come from more taxation or from more spending. It will come from the collective power of the people, not a powerful collection of politicians.

With the power of the people, change for the better does come. We have examples on both sides of the political aisle throughout American history.

Ronald Reagan started his presidential campaign in Philadelphia, Mississippi, a town historically marred by a low point in the Civil Rights fight. Yet, it was the same man – later as President Reagan – that signed into law the Martin Luther King national holiday that we celebrate today.

The Democratic Party was the party that fought for segregation against African-Americans throughout the Civil Rights era of the 20th century. Yet, it was that same Democratic Party that nominated, then supported the first Black president of the United States.

So yes, change does comes, but it only comes through the persistence of the people - people that work through obstacles of name-calling, disenfranchisement, and discouragement from the status quo to remind us of what is right, what is best, and what is American.

Tea Party people today: with your protests against the outrageous spending that is burdening our children and grandchildren with global debt, you are reminding us of doing what is right.

With your demands that we return the government to the will of the people through smaller, representative government that fosters bigger opportunities for everyday Americans, you are reminding us of what is best.

With your persistence to make your voices heard again and again, regardless of race, gender, socioeconomics, political affiliation, or location, you are reminding us of what is truly American.

You exemplify freedom of assembly. You extol the merits of freedom of speech. You make possible the freedom to prosper.

You are reminding us of what is truly American at a time when the leadership in Washington continues to moves us past a point of recognizing what made this nation so great for so many years.

We now see the desire to be popular with our enemies overseas and be seen as fair by those that attack Americans supersede the obligation of our president and his administration to put the safety of the American people first and foremost. It is time for us – the people of the United States – to remind our elected leadership in Washington that while understanding the human rights of terrorists may hold ethical merit, upholding civil rights of terrorists is unfounded at a time when giving terrorists American criminal rights in court is more important to this administration than getting the needed information to keep Americans safe in the war on terror.

2010 is the year to say clearly and continuously:

Mr. President – prioritize protecting Americans over protecting your reputation around the world.

Mr. President – the prize of a peaceful and safe American homeland will always be worth more than your Nobel Peace Prize.

Mr. President – allow us to claim victory in this war on terror without any campaign timetables before the terrorists claim any more lives.

Mr. President – you are called to be a commander-in-chief to protect our homeland from these attacks, not be a commander-in-thief in taking the nation into unmanageable debt with unsuccessful stimulus packages, cash-for-clunker schemes to uphold the broken and stubborn business model of American automakers, and a questionable national health care plan while unemployment stays unbearable and everyday Americans stay anxious about their prospects for recovery.

We cannot and will not spend our way out of this recession. Big government spending never solved our problems. American brainpower and elbow grease always have.

And that is why it is up to us.

It is up to us, fellow patriots, to remind our government that spending our tax dollars to give us more only ensures us that our government will come around for more of our tax dollars. Taxation does not ensure the prosperity of a nation. Innovation does. Commitment does. Education does. Emancipation of the people does.

Yet, we have watched billions given to banks that asked for money to unfreeze the credit market for Americans, only to watch them freeze out everyday Americans from the rebound that Wall Street experienced over the past several months. Banks have played a corrupt game of us versus them in American business, just as American career politicians have played a continuing game of us versus them in American politics for years.

It is up to us, fellow patriots – today and now – to tell these businesses that horde American prosperity with off-shoring and outsourcing during good times and taxpayer-funded bailouts during bad times that the American taxpayer is not a pawn in your personal game of greed. Without hardworking Americans to pay your goods, Mr. AIG, you are good for nothing. Everyday Americans – and their children and grandchildren – bailed you out of your mire of greed and dysfunction that led to the financial crisis, only for you to spend it on bonuses based on your incompetence. Now it is time for you to work to beat back the rising rate of unemployment. Your profit margins can only be maximized through optimizing American prosperity – and that comes only through American jobs, American workers, and American products being made in the United States of America, sold throughout the world, and winning in the global markets just as we have done for decades. I believe in the American worker – it is time that you believe in him again as well.

Big and unresponsive government restricts American workmanship. Efficient and representative government empowers it – and protects us and our prosperity. We have the talent and the willpower. I believe in the USA. It is our time to make sure that our government acts that way as well.

It is up to us, fellow patriots – today and now – to tell these politicians that our history of republican government of the people is not a roadmap for their individual fame and glory, but a structure guiding the freedom and prosperity for a nation of millions. The 4 walls of government were not built for their comfort in making illicit backroom deals to pass billion-dollar legislation with diminishing benefits for the American people. Those rooms are to be used to empower American ingenuity, encourage private solutions without increased government limitations, and invigorate the economic, social, and personal wealth of Americans – not entrench career politicians into office, particularly those that have forgotten that they serve the American people, not the other way around. It is up to us to say to these politicians in 2010 – change is going to come. Either you will change your ways of spending and of handling the business of government starting in January, or you will be surely be changing your location of business after November.

It is up to us, fellow patriots, to do more than just protest, however. Just as Dr. King did, we must protest and be proactive – we must dream while being diligent with our desires. As a politician, I could tell you what party to be involved with, but as an American, I must implore you to be involved regardless of party affiliation. The mindless servant of politics is the person that does not have an active constituency to be mindful of. That part is up to us today – we must be mindful of our role to stay active in the process if we expect the political process and its participants to stay mindful of our high standards and our historical obligations between government and those that truly govern – we the people of the United States.

Be not discouraged, patriots. This seems like a daunting task, but Americans have faced grim realities before throughout our history and have always created greater realities for themselves in the end.

Only in the United States of America can the rich run for the highest offices of the land, only to be defeated at the hands of the poorest voters at the polls. America was never about the royalty of a few but the prosperity of a nation. With your efforts in elections, in town hall meetings, in local government debates, and in building alliances with your neighbors every day, you can reincorporate the everyday American into the fabric of politics every day. A government focused on taxing and spending is solely concerned about your money. A nation focused on your talents and liberty is focused on your patriotism, your desire to work hard and contribute, and your ability to rebuild America. With you, we make our country less about our government and more about our countrymen and women, the people that our government works for.

Only in the United States of America can the competition of business ideas, the competition of schools and their offerings, and the competition of products across state lines make for a better overall system for us all. We embrace diversity, we encourage healthy debate, and we foster a way of life that says that no one group should dominate based on numbers alone, but should lead with the best ideas and the best models for leadership. Health care reform should not come in America by

way of the Democrats have 60 senators; it must come through the sharing of bipartisan ideas that embrace the American spirit of competition of choice, business innovation to drive down cost, and the knowledge that government that dictates how to provide health care can also decide when health care is no longer available based on bureaucratic urges and statistical conclusions.

Freedom – whether it is in health care, in educational opportunities, or from societal restraints – can never be taxed and sold, nor can it be purchased in backroom deals and corrupt conference meetings. It is earned with our patriotism. It is earned with our engagement with the issues. It is bonded with our love for every good thing that America stands for as a unique presence in the world. It is through that promise of hope – not the false promise of free health care – that America shines as the city on a hill throughout the global community.

American health care reform will not come from taxation in 2010 without implementation for years down the road. The sanctity of life is too precious for that, despite what Mr. Reid and Ms. Pelosi will tell you. Health care reform will come from listening to the American people and giving us what we want – more control of our choices, less costs for service and goods, and the same quality of access and care that we enjoy today. Freedom of choice and quality of service will only be gained the same way as it always has been – through free market enterprise…the beauty of the American way of life.

It is up to us, fellow patriots, to be the change that we can believe in, not the lack of change that we have seen in Washington. It is up to us, fellow Americans, to be the primers of change through our willingness to protest and educate and through our persistence to be involved and be heard. Being a rabble-rouser or being on television means nothing if we are not then ready to be a force with our representatives in Washington, Tallahassee, and points of government in between.

We celebrate the accomplishments of Dr. Martin Luther King, Jr. today because he was willing to be historic at a time when doing so was a threat against his life.

We protest today against the efforts of a tax-and-spend, minimally-effective government because of its threats against our liberty.

We must dare to be historic today and throughout 2010 because without our constant action as respectful activists, candidates, speakers, and citizens, we incur a major obstacle in our collective pursuit of happiness.

The Constitution calls on us to be amenable to these inalienable rights, but the times call on us to be historic to protect these inalienable rights. As I have mentioned in my book, America is in need of recovering through smaller government and bigger people. That means that **you** are the giants that our nation needs to stop the gigantic debt mounting in Washington. **You** are the giants that we need to raise the accountability to stop the huge push for a system of change that America has not bargained for. **You** are the giants to rein in a system that stopped listening to America previously, but now hears your voices loud and clear today.

Be the change.

Be historic.

Be not afraid and be not deterred.

In the face of civil rights challenges, Dr. King was a giant that overcame the negativity, name-calling, and discouragement to beat back government and provide a better way for us all in the 20th century.

In the face of mounting personal restrictions and intense debt, you are the giants to overcome the name-calling and discouragement to beat back government into its rightful place and provide a better way for us all in the 21st century.

So I say:

Be historic.

Be the change.

Be what Dr. King was before you: a protesting patriot with a vision for tomorrow, an unyielding passion for America and equality, and a refusal to stop until life, liberty, and the pursuit of happiness was once again safe and sound in America in his time.

This is now our calling and this is now our time. Let's do this – together.

Let's be historic. What do you say? Are you with me?

The time is now. Let's be historic.

Thank you for this opportunity. Stay involved with what you do. God Bless you all and God Bless the United States of America.

Lenny McAllister: Carolina Sweet Tea Party
2009 April 3 ("**Social Responsibility and American Ambassadors**")

Good morning. Thank you for having me this morning. More importantly, I want to thank you for taking the time to protest the direction you see our country moving in.

Now, we all know that the ability to protest in a country where our voice is heard in City Hall, Raleigh North Carolina, and Washington DC is a dear right that we have because of the sacrifices of other proud Americans. Because we honor the gift of freedom, it is our responsibility to speak up and ensure that our voices are reflected in our government because the power of our republic…calls for the involvement *of* the republic – namely, the citizens of the United States of America, speaking up in the best interests of our future.

We also know that being involved in a protest takes on two components. Each component comes from parts of the word "protest."

First, let's look at the prefix "pro." PRO. It means "forward." It means "in favor of." It stands for development and positivity. So, when we come together to protest the direction of our country – expansive government as well as EXPENSIVE government – we come together not to complain about America, but to forward the American Dream. We are not merely against the president's budget or the governor's plans - we are in favor of the most efficient, most practical, and most successful actions for the future of North Carolina and of the United States. We criticize to be constructive. We are proactive to move forward to a better America for her citizens.

The second part of the word "protest" is "test." It means to validate. It means to assess. It means to examine. So, when we come together to protest and examine the direction our elected officials are taking us in, we must also validate, assess, and examine our positions and actions as well, from our votes putting these officials into office to our efforts furthering the best interests of our communities.

Many object to what is called an increased socialist interpretation of government's role in our lives. Today, I ask for us today to make it an *objective* to take a more social interpretation of the citizen's role in our lives.

Every November, we have a chance to vote against a socialist agenda, but every day, we have a chance to choose a higher social awareness, because until we can vote to express our feelings on increasing the deficit and out of control spending, we must focus on how we spend our time and our energy to close the deficits in our schools and communities.

We can grow America stronger even in the face of budgets that grow more expensive…and government that grows more expansive until we can change the face of our government.

A socialist, larger government approach focuses on the power of the government. A social awareness that we call for today focuses on the power of you, the people. Our great constitution does not start with "we the government." It proudly – and correctly – states "we the people."

And that is what we must do in order to turn around this great

country. Protest – Pro…to forward or be in favor of. Test…to examine.

Therefore, we must examine what we – the people - can do. We must move forward with what we can do, putting it into motion immediately. We must be in favor of the American Way, even as we protest the way America is going.

So, what can we do in order to better our country?

First, we must learn more about the community around us all of the time – no excuses. Many have used brawn and backbone to defend this country. Therefore, we must use our minds to improve this country.

Everyday Americans must value education of our policies, of our budgets, of our rights, and of our laws. Everyday Americans must enthusiastically learn more about the price of freedom that we enjoy, from the sacrifices of our servicemen and women to the foresight of our forefathers to create a republic that values a responsive and representative government that values *serving* us, not ruling us or just taxing us.

Everyday Americans must invest in the gift of citizenry, knowing that it is a gift fought for, a gift that grows with each American accomplishment, and a gift that grows in importance as we face a runaway political and social mentality that falsely believes that bigger is better, that more money guarantees more success, and that more government is more American.

Everyday Americans must know in our hearts that government is for the people, **not** the other way around. It is time to bring politics back to the people, and it will take all of us as ambassadors of that message to temper the government spending, government expansion, and government impropriety that threatens our quality of life and our ability as We the People to improve America.

To make the United States a more perfect Union despite our current situation and subsequent outcry, we must live our political and social rhetoric in real life, and not continue to jam real life into the canned packaging of our rhetoric. Our failure to move our energy from emotionalism to activism is an American crisis that no stimulus money, bank bailout, nor government program will ever fix.

Starting today, we must provide the **sound leadership** on the ground and in our communities so that we can change the **sound bite mentality** of politicians that sell us down a dangerous political path of increased debt and decreased emphasis on the individual American citizen.

It is your sound leadership being voiced today that will make both sides put into motion…what their mouths say.

In protest, we can not testify about compassionate conservatism if we are not willing to do the work to show our compassion with tangible actions that successfully replace the failed social programs in our cities since the 1960s. We are not compassionate conservatives if we are not successfully engaging and incorporating everyday Americans from all walks of life.

As well, there can be no testimony of protest from loving liberals if they are willing to demonize a significant portion of patriotic Americans based on politics alone. One can not claim to be a loving and enlightened liberal while offering an expectation of life that gravitates primarily around the government as the center of one's universe, not one's own self as the center of one's own powerful destiny as a child of God.

Walking the talk for all of us starts with uplifting our children – the students of today and the leaders of tomorrow.

Our goal to empower them will be fulfilled with the involvement of parents, the support of the community, and with the enforcement of morals and standards within the schools – by adults of all walks of life. Our schools will turn around primarily through the human touch, not through the color of money. Increased taxes and increased spending on an unchanging educational system that is increasingly failing more students with each passing day is akin to paying for a brand new Lincoln Towncar and only getting a Ford Pinto. It may get you to where you are going, but barely, and it does not provide the class, accomplishment, and reliability that you will need for the long journeys ahead.

For every $1 worth of school spending that we see, we will need $10 of volunteer tutoring. We will need $10 of volunteer time. We will need $10 of parental involvement with your children. We will need $10 of lunch buddies. We will need $10 of library time, of donated books, of being an academic role model to your children and to your children's friends when you see them. This is something that you can give starting today but it's something that you can never pay for. No increase in spending can provide what our children really need – **Y-O-U**.

The children of America are in crisis – from the growing national deficit that they are inheriting to the education that they are not receiving. A big budget may procure them books but the ambassadors here today that get involved– all of you – will procure their education. And by procuring their education, you are securing America's future.

And be not afraid. Now is the time. Unemployed does not need to mean unengaged. Hunting for job security does not need to mean hiding from the greater call before you. The lessons that our children need to learn to lead in the 21st century will come from our rightful responses to adversity, to obstacles, and to naysayers. Show them that you can protest historic taxation and spending and still share in the triumph of a renewed America. Now is the time to say to them – and show them – "yes we can" – showing them that campaign rhetoric is never as good as creating that new reality.

While we tackle the education issue head-on…with our minds and not just our wallets…we can also tackle violence in our communities…and the destruction of resources, talents, and lives that it brings.

We will allow our police forces to deal directly with street criminals…as we deal with the indivisible crime right before our eyes. The indivisible plague of domestic violence is a drain on money, communities, and families – a plague that we can eliminate starting today through the expression of one mantra continuously:

We will not accept the existence of partner abuse in our communities because it is a price that all of us can not afford to pay any longer.

We can not afford the $700 million in business productivity lost annually due to domestic violence as we compete on a global scale in a tough economy.

We can not afford to have our police departments spend the majority of their calls on domestic situations if we plan on cleaning up our streets of illegal guns, illegal drugs, and illegal activity.

We can not afford to show our young ladies and gentlemen that violent control is love and that abusive behavior is acceptable if we are going to be the ambassadors to usher in the new era of the

2-parent American family for our children and grandchildren.

We can not tolerate condoning domestic violence in our churches, in our courtrooms, in our corporate settings, and in our communities regardless of race or gender. And as an ambassador to bring about change without having you spend more of your change, display your opposition to a preventable violence – domestic violence. Save us money even as we protest more spending. More importantly, someone you love may be counting on it and America and her children will certainly thank you for it.

Fellow ambassadors...fellow Americans. These are some things that we can do to make a difference without increasing spending. I trust your creativity, your investment in America, and your love of our country and our neighbors, so I know that you will continue to search for newer, better ways to take America higher and not take Americans into higher amounts of spending, taxation, and debt. Just spending more money on our schools and our communities will never have the same impact as spending time in our schools and in our communities. Building out the American government will never be as powerful or successful as embracing the power **IN**...the American people.

Yes, there is change that we can believe in, but it will never come from a politician or a government program. It will never come from more taxation or from more spending. It will come from bringing politics back to the people because we are a government of "We the People."

It is time to reel in spending. It is time to reel in government.

It is time to roll out the era of the new, educated, engaged, and energized American citizen.

Ambassadors, it is your time.

Thank you for this opportunity. God Bless this great state of North Carolina and God Bless the United States of America.

Lenny McAllister: Bainbridge, GA
2010 April 15 ("**The TEA Party Must Mean More than Just Taxed Enough Already**")

Good afternoon, Bainbridge Tea Party Patriots!

Thank you for welcoming me into your wonderful town. Thank you for offering me a chance to speak to you this afternoon.

Already, in just this short period of time, we have already shut down a few stereotypes about hard-working, God-fearing, American-loving tea party patriots:

One – that Black people are not willing to come to a tea party.

Two – that there are no tea party patriots willing to invite Black people to a tea party.

Three – that our love for America can prompt us to act with pride, not hate.

So, let me clarify for anyone willing to protest out of malice to derail this historic populist movement to take government in America back to the constructs of the Constitution: this Tea Party – and tea parties around the nation – will not tolerate your hatred, buy into your distractions, and will not be stopped until government goes back to the primary focus of serving the American people, not its own selfish gain.

And let me be clear: there is a lot that our governments – at the local, state, and federal levels – have gained out of selfish focus and failure to understand the premise of "We the People." There has been a health care bill passed without the will of the majority of Americans because a small majority of politicians in Washington thought they knew what was best. I know that there were politicians from my home state of North Carolina that disregarded our protests and phone calls, just as there are politicians such as Representative Sanford Bishop here in Georgia that did the same. When the vast majority of your constituents are against legislation that is being presented, as a representative of the people, there is an obligation to engage, listen to, and represent the people of the district that one serves, not one's friends in high places. Big time Washington politics should never trump the needs of small town American values – and when it does, it is time for big time Washington politicians to be retired from politics and brought back home as a reminder of who is in charge.

From Bainbridge, Georgia to Boston, Massachusetts, this must be the rallying call today: it is time to be historic. The first revolutionary war was fought by a small but growing minority of colonists that understood the history-making opportunity before  them. This second revolutionary war – the one being fought by patriots such as all of you here today – is being carried on by a growing minority of Americans that understand that we must defend the gains of the past centuries of American law if we are going to bequeath to our children and grandchildren the greatness of the United States of America.

Our mantra as a movement started with the phrase "taxed enough already." That is not enough today. With the legislative directives coming from Washington, DC…with the questionable moves that we see from the White House with traditional allies such as France and Israel…with the express desire to skirt the Constitution and redistribute the wealth…we must continue not the T-E-A Party…Taxed Enough Already…we must move forward with the T-B-A Party: Taking Back America.

Now, what does that mean, Bainbridge? Are we referring to taking back America from a Black president or from Latino-Americans or from professional American women?

I say clearly and loudly: no. This is not about race, gender, or ethnicity. Anyone that thinks that our movement to take back America from a legitimate culture group within America does not understand the power and the glory that God has bestowed on our great nation through the melting pot that we embrace. Anyone that believes that this is about hatred does not believe in the inscription found in the Statue of Liberty. We do not hate the poor: we embrace them as they work to become the prosperous. The huddle masses yearning to breathe free are also the ones that will fight to the last breath to ensure that the government that oversees our nation will not tax us – or legislate us – to death. Like Lady Liberty, we seek not to be a dark cloud on America, but the T-E-A Party *and* the TBA Party – seek to be a new light in America, shining the way to a path of opportunity, a land of prosperity, and a national community of leaders that embrace the Constitution and the ability to live free under its protection.

71

Taking back America means taking up the lamp of liberty on behalf of those that fought this good fight before us – and for those that seek to ensure that there is an America to give to generations after us.

The America that will come after we are long since gone must honor farmers in Georgia the same way it supports computer programmers in Granada Hills, California or, for that matter, meat-packers in Green Bay, Wisconsin and laborers in Gary, Indiana. Cap-and-trade must not be allowed to have a chance to cap our ability to prosper in the small towns and small businesses of everyday America. Cap-and-trade must not be given the leeway to trade away our ability to compete globally with nations that do not value these agreements the same way that we do. It may not be socialist or communist to put such agreements into place, but I say with respect but with candor: any president or congressman that puts an American cap-and-trade law into place, knowing that other nations within the global economy will NOT obey the same rules of business engagement, is being un-American. THAT is something that we have to take our nation back from.

Patriots, what we face is more than just being "taxed enough already". It is no longer just about TEA. It is about TBA – taking back America.

It is about taking back our nation from the misguided philosophy that we can spend our way out of this economic mess from the top. Anytime Christina Romer, the chair of the White House Council of Economic Advisers, tells us in December that government spending is a "sensible policy" to get us out of a recession – only to tell us months later that there is only so much government can do in order to end this recession through its spending – we know that we need a change.

After hearing that, it is clear: yes, Madam Chair…and yes, Mr. President….we need a change…a necessary change that we can believe in…and it is not the change in our pockets from your additional, misguided spending…it appears to be a necessary change in Washington leadership, starting in 2010 this November and onward to 2012 and the White House.

And why do we advocate such a historic change in 2010 and 2012 soon after the historic election of 2008?

It is because we cannot allow for another financial farce to occur on behalf of the American people as we have seen with the stimulus package. Legislation that was rushed through votes along party lines under the guise that unemployment would be capped at 8% nationally with swift action on Capitol Hill.

Capped at 8%, huh? I'd love to trade that capped number instead of having the 10% unemployment we have suffered around the nation over the past year or so, right? That's the only cap-and-trade the American people need at this point, not another job-killing bill, right?

The stimulus package is enough to question the direction of the nation. Yet, that is not all that push us from being a party that is T-E-A to a force that is T-B-A.

When our president says on national television that he is not worried about the legislative process that guides the formation of our laws – we must conclude that we have a nation to take back.

When we hear congressmen say on the internet that he is not worried about the Constitution when it comes to Obamacare and other votes such as reconciliation and procedure tactics in order to win on Capitol Hill – not vote in accordance of representing their constituents – then we must conclude that we have a nation to take back.

When we see that education is failing in our nation as-is, but people want to fund it more as-is: we have a nation to take back.

When we see jobs failing to come back into the economy, even as Wall Street and banks such as JP Morgan Chase flourish with $3.3 billion profits reports this past quarter – all while the federal government TARPs them out of trouble as they refuse to loan small businesses back to recovery – folks, we have a nation to take back.

The move towards socialism at the top of the government structure in America threatens the republican form of government in the small towns of everyday America. If we merely focus on being a T-E-A Party, we will not be successful. If we believe that we are T-B-A Movement, we will overcome – just as we did in the 1800s and the 1900s.

This movement – the T-B-A Movement – is about smaller government, bigger people. We must be willing to take a bigger role in the formation of our government, the efficiency of our government, and the prosperity of our nation. We must understand, promote, and support the notion that America is the land where dreams come true - the American Dream – not through the subsidized plans of a government bureaucracy, but through the hard work and American ingenuity of its citizen leaders, willing to fight for their rights and work for a better way.

Now is the time to be historic, patriots. People will attempt to distraction us with different slights and accusations. They will call us racists. They will call us sexists. They will call us hateful. They will call us misguided. They will call us inappropriate. They will call us failures.

They said the same thing about General Washington before he became President Washington and formed a nation.

They said the same thing about a short preacher – a native Georgian named Martin King - until he was given the Nobel Peace Prize and changed a nation.

They said the same thing about a former actor named Ronnie Reagan and his fight to end communism's threat throughout the world until a little wall in Berlin fell – per his request – along with the fall of the former Soviet Union.

They said the same thing about the efforts to battle back Hitler in the 1940s and defeat Britain in the 1770s. They said the same thing about coming back as a world economic force in the 1890s and the 1930s.

Yet, in each instance, we have not been failures. In each instance, we have been victors. In each instance, we have been leaders for prosperity in America and for the rest of the world.

Just the same, we are not failures as members of the T-B-A Party. We will be victors within the 21st century for a stronger, better America, just as our forefathers were in the centuries before us.

Americanism wins when we embrace it. The United States leads when it is viewed as a force of good. The Constitution defeats tyranny whenever it is used as an instrument of justice.

Now is the time to take up this mantle, and when we find that America- or American politicians – are unwilling or unable to take up this historical mantle and bring about us back to the historical honor that proud Americans forged for us in our past, we must be the patriots willing to fight today to uphold this great land and the promise it represents as a God-fearing, freedom-loving land of self-determination.

Complaining about being "taxed enough already" is plenty when seen in the context of congressmen supporting job-killing and tax-expanding legislation such has cap-and-trade, the health care legislation, and the stimulus package that will come back to tax more hard-working Americans. However, we must speak to taking back America if we are going to be victorious in the broader sense. This is more than just reducing the tax burden on everyday Americans, fellow patriots. This is about increasing the amount of prosperity and freedom in America. This is about having laws in place that allow our citizens to touch the American Dream and own their destiny in our nation. This is about having politicians in place that lead with humble, servant leadership – not politicians that vote for cap-and-trade against the will of the people, vote for installing government-based health care plans against the will of the people, and support reconciliation in order to skirt the basic tenets of procedure in Congress. This movement is about having a financial, constitutional, and community freedom for current and future Americans.

Thank you for this opportunity to speak to you today. God Bless you all and God Bless the United States of America.

Lenny McAllister: Illinois Tax Day Revolt
2011 April 15 ("**A Party for Touting Exceptionalism in America**")

Good afternoon, my fellow Illinoisans. Hello, my fellow Americans. Thank you for having me this afternoon. More importantly, thank you for saying collectively and loudly: we love America, we believe in America, and we know that with a focused effort by 21st century local, state, and federal leaders from the grassroots to the General Assembly – we will see the resurgence of a fiscally, socially, and economically strong America for many generations to come.

Let me also say thank you to Rhonda Linders and her team for their invitation and support to make it possible for me to be here today. Thanks to the Northern Illinois Patriots and the Chicago Tea Party for both their hospitality at their recent monthly meetings as well as their invitation to allow me to speak to the fine Americans that will gather in Daley Plaza in downtown Chicago on April 18th.

We come here to Springfield, Illinois today, gathering together to make a big deal over a big tax hike at a rather paramount moment in the history of our state and of our nation. Particularly in Illinois, it is becoming quite clear that anytime a huge tax hike in the Land of Lincoln is enough to make a big shot governor in New Jersey…(or should I say "big-boned" governor in New Jersey…) anytime the big man in New Jersey is making a large plea to Illinois-based businesses to make a grand move from our state to his…folks, you know that we have a huge problem that we must address immediately with no small delay.

So we come here today despite the slander and slurs thrown out about us and against us regularly. We come here today to speak above the fray of distractions to reclaim the harmony our nation deserves. I say thank you – thank you to those that have supported my efforts to take our message to the masses and thank you to those that come to the state capital today on the path of taking our mission to another level, even as we have to maintain overcoming the distracting false accusations of being hateful, being racist, being misguided, and being misinformed.

So, today, we look to continue putting America back on the track of prosperity even as we also set aside those undue items of criticism to say loudly and clearly:

You accuse us of being hateful. Well, yes, we are hateful, but not in the way that you suggest.

See, we hate that special interest groups have dictated to elected officials for decades that the way to make government function is by making government spend more – even if that means serving the people it represents less and less with each dollar spent. We hate that politicians are more willing to demonize conservative activists than they are to de-fund special interest programs or reduce the inefficiencies of bureaucracy that strangle the breath out of the American Dream for working class people that seek to advance themselves and their families through this Great Recession and into our next great era of prominence.

We are here today to declare without equivocation: we seek to inspire revolutionary change for a better future for all Americans, not a return to the racism of the past that restricted the potential of all Americans. Our movement understands that with greater efficiency from government and lowered economic inhibitors by government, more Americans can be empowered past their current conditions into the promise of their individual dreams, a vision that supersedes even the oppressive economic mandates given by the legislative towers in Springfield to the 4 corners of the Land of Lincoln.

We understand that smaller government must mean bigger people, and that with bigger people come greater people from all walks of life, from all creeds and colors – and with them all professing the United States of America as their home…with them proclaiming the USA as the protector of their rights and opportunities as afforded by God, not government…and with them upholding the America that serves as the Shining City on a Hill for the world to see, just as the patriots before us fought for from battlefields to hearts and minds everywhere.

We are here to ask of those that call us misinformed and misguided when we say that our national debt and runaway love affair with taxation and bureaucracy threaten the freedoms we hold as citizens…we ask this: explain to us your path to liberating and refreshing sovereignty based on this current trend of doing business in America.

But before you answer, simply remember: we have seen your path. It leads to exploding debt, suffocating bureaucracy, and self-serving government. We know our path. Simply put: it leads to freedom.

We know that to be a truly sovereign nation, the United States must have a resurgence of economic freedom, personal vitality, and national perseverance that allows us as a people to have a rebuilt, re-calibrated, and re-emboldened moral compass and civic backbone. It is impossible to encourage that resurgence of the shoulders-back, heads-held-high, forthright American consciousness when we are constantly taxing our citizens into submission and chasing businesses from our communities because of politicians' collective failure to act as leaders before the procrastinated decisions of yesterday became our shared crisis today.

Furthermore, we cannot have the sturdy and straight backbone of a strong and sovereign nation if we must always bend over and gravel at the feet of our foreign debtors to borrow more money, buy more imported oil, and use more outsourced workers because of our inability to enact fiscal discipline, our failure to envision economic and civic solutions to compete globally, and our unwillingness to trust the power of the American people and unchain the ingenuity and diligence of the nation's citizens.

At a time when America is challenged domestically by harrowing disparities between fellow citizens within the realms of education, economic opportunities, and quality of life …and at a time when America is threatened internationally by radical terrorists and oppressive regimes alike…we cannot uphold the tenets of the American Dream within our borders and around the world if we continue to jack up and justify our debt, even as we simultaneously squander away the resources we do have through expansive government and expensive bureaucracy.

We are weakened in our ability to withstand the auspices of socialism and secularism…of radicalism abroad and rolling back the clock to more divisive and hypocritical times here at home…if we continue to tolerate our inclination to increase debt ceilings and decrease opportunities in America for Americans. This trend merely whittles away the hopes of future generations of Americans both Black and White, both working class and legacy class, both men and women – for the lost freedom to achieve and succeed for everyday Americans is the millstone that drowns the aspirations of well-to-do Americans to be leaders with a legacy of honor, not leeches feeding off of the struggles of their fellow countrymen. Americans of all creeds and colors deserve each day to have the ability to pursue happiness and reach for prosperity. Tea Party Americans of all creeds and colors are the lifeblood of a movement to re-establish that expectation for our children and grandchildren starting now.

We understand that the resurgence of the American republic has no roots solely in a politician or his select candidates that will bring us change we can believe in or hope that we can change, even when Main Street continues to struggle, even after Wall Street was bailed out on Main Street's dime. We know that American partisan politics will never save this nation – only forthright American leadership will.

We know that American leadership on Capitol Hill today and in Springfield in the days to come yields results only when the representative government is held accountable to those they serve in office – we the people of this state and of this nation. We know that without our presence here today and our movement over the past several years, opportunities would continue to be squandered and America as we know it would soon cease to exist.

Some will come to us and say that we must trust the president and the governor more and give them more time to build their cases for prosperity. In reply, I say today:

If a president and his political movement and allies can come to power in Washington and Springfield with historic political capital, global affection, and wide-sweeping potential, only to let the political and ethical high-ground seep away because a rushed stimulus package that failed to keep unemployment at 8%...if that post-partisan change can be fumbled away through an unconstitutional and costly health care package that wishes to tax Americans into purchasing decisions for the first time in American history after a series of political bribes in Congress that excluded your desires as constituents but included Cornhusker Kickbacks and Louisiana Purchases....if hope for a better way for all Americans can become disturbingly silent on issues of race relations after garnering 98% of the Black vote while simultaneously speaking up for the residency rights of illegal immigrants in America and the civil rights for terroristic and murderous enemies of America...if the political argument of demagogy against funding a war in Iraq becomes lost while delaying an explanation on why we are now funding a third war effort in Libya at a time when we cut funding for college students in America, ask to raise taxes on job creators in America, yet continue funding abortion services both domestically and internationally with American tax dollars during a time of great deficit....

If this political capital...this political currency, if you will...if it can be wasted so questionably and so tragically over such a short period of time...what do you think would happen to tax dollars both in Washington, DC and in Springfield, IL if runaway spending and debt are allowed to remain unbridled under that type of political leadership– whether it would be expressed through fully implementing Obamacare or fully embracing the recent new tax culture here in Illinois?

In the darkness of night, Governor Quinn and his political allies showed the people of Illinois their willingness to forfeit the future through lack of vision today to pay for the mismanagement of the distant and recent past. In the shadow of a supermajority in Washington, President Obama and his political allies showed Illinois and America their willingness to discard the need to put America back on the track of fiscal responsibility and economic and employment vitality for the sake of political philosophy.

We are not misguided and we are not misinformed. We have merely been misrepresented by the political powers that be for far too long – and the time for that to end is now.

We have seen the yield of this failure in leadership for years now by self-serving politicians from both sides of the aisle. The brink of bankruptcy is borne from years of big government and redundant bureaucracy… from believing that the way they've always done it in government is the way we should always do it in government, even if it drives us off of the fiscal cliff. It comes from not having a big enough vision to see a brighter future for our state and the State of our Union without big government – and ultimately even Big Brother – being a part in every aspect of our lives.

Yet at a time when apathy ran roughshod across America, your activism sparked accountability on both sides of the political aisle. It is only through your activism and angst – a frustration that started in 2006 and overflowed in 2009 – that you came together and you said today and henceforth:

No longer are we going to sit by and watch folks spend away the American Dream from their perch in Washington and here in Springfield.
Not on our watch any longer, gentlemen…and not on our dime.

We were apathetic as a nation before, but now…

We are awake. We are paying attention. And we will not rest until we take back America.

We are here not to just honor America's history. We are here today in the effort to make American history – and not just to make history, but to make the right type of history.

Blind adherence to the ways of the past without the flexibility of vision is symptomatic of the political mainstream, not a characteristic of American leadership. For example, President Obama noted on Wednesday that "…wealthier individuals have traditionally born a greater share of the tax burden than the middle class or those less fortunate." Sadly, he slipped into believing and promoting the model that what was done in previous times must continue to be done today. By that model, traditionally…from 1619 until the middle of the 20th century, Black people in the United States were either state-sanctioned second-class citizens or flat-out slaves. As we gather proudly in the Land of Lincoln – the land of the Great Emancipator – we stand and remind the president humbly but clearly: the only tradition that we must uphold in America is freedom – for people, for prosperity, and for the pursuit of happiness mentioned in the Declaration of Independence.

We are here to take back America from the brink of losing its sovereignty to the self-serving existence of unresponsive government that ignores the Constitution and the law in order to continue its personal gravy train. We are here to take back America from the clutches of the dictatorship of foreign debt to nations that believe in telling its citizens how many children to have per family by law and restraining the access of its citizens to facts and free speech by way of government oppression.

However, we are here to do even more.

We are here to extol the rebirth of American Exceptionalism, a concept lost on too many of our politicians in sanctuary cities and capital cities across the nation. We understand that economic freedom as a nation affords us more breathing room to stand for the beauty of humble but meaningful expression of the power captured within American Exceptionalism. We know that we find ourselves at a time in our nation's history where we are required us to stand for fiscal correction at the local, state, and federal levels, but we also know that we stand at a point where our historical obligations to past patriots of all creeds demand that we exude leadership that doles out belief in American Exceptionalism, not apologies for America to other nations at the drop of our handout hat with the need to borrow more money.

Our task yesterday was just to request and require that over-taxation and over-spending cease through the Taxed Enough Already Party momentum. Our task today and beyond is to improve all aspects of America through a new TEA Party

Movement – a T-E-A Party Movement that Touts the Exceptionalism of America.

Yes, we should – and we must – take back America through touting the exceptionalism of America, but this must be done through embracing the potential for exceptionalism within **all** aspects of America. Without finding big potential in all things American, we will never be able to beat back big government and big spending in America.

We are here today to take back America, but we can never successfully take back America until we are successful in taking back urban America and the youth in America. The patriots fighting for fiscal correctness in California will never be successful if they refuse to battle the conditions that lead to government reliance in Compton, California with the same fervor they have in the state's capital. The Tea Party Patriots protesting the scope of government in the Land of Dixie will never find victory if they will not engage the social conditions that expand government bureaucracy in Atlanta and Decatur, Georgia. Just the same, we cannot expect to find fiscal sanity here in the Land of Lincoln from Carbondale to Elgin if we collectively continue to tolerate the insanity found on the streets of south Chicago and in East St. Louis, Illinois.

The onslaught on American sovereignty both domestically and globally through the collective fiscal crisis encountered at all civic levels throughout the nation cannot be overcome without overturning the slaughter of America's youth in the violent streets of our communities and through the abominations of waste and unprofessionalism that collectively masquerade as our educational system and standards for our children.

Not only should we not even attempt to take back America without looking at this whole picture – we could not do it, even if we tried, regardless of our passion or patriotism. The honesty found within the ideal sense of American Exceptionalism will not allow us to do so.

Big government, big taxation and big bureaucracy believe in the Great Society – a movement that has failed us all through the trials and tribulations of social engineering. The role of smaller government and the role of bigger people in America believe instead...in the pursuit and protection of social equality in America, where it is better for the American people – through caring, innovation, and desire – to put their time and resources where their faith in America is without unnecessary interference. And we believe that it is only through the American people taking the lead to improve our economic and employment situations as well as our neighborhoods and communities can we truly take back America.

This is why our radio station in Chicago – WVON 1690 AM – went out of our way to raise over $60,000 for the young people of the Martin Luther King, Jr. Boys and Girls Club of Chicago. We knew that if we waited for government to do right on behalf of the young people that needed it the most, we risked more causalities to ad nauseam bureaucracy, fed on by ad nauseam government spending – all with diminishing results for the people that need it the most.

That is why I feel so comfortable in asking my fellow conservative political commentators to follow WVON's lead. I'm asking the Glenn Becks and Rush Limbaughs of the political media landscape – those that can easily afford to match our $60,000 accomplishment – to join us immediately in aiding the efforts of those working to take back America in the broadest sense, be it in Chicago with the Boys and Girls Club or with other similar organizations. With this effort, we can remind the government once again: a strong society of empowered citizens does not come from government-guided social engineering that is empowered by big taxation. It comes from embracing the Constitution, enforcing equality, and reintroducing American Exceptionalism from Harlem to Beverly Hills. With a strong and consolidated effort, we can together resonate the time-tested message that we purport again today: that the liberal agenda of taxing-and-spending has never had a liberating effect on the inner cities of our nation nor for the struggling Americans that cannot escape the perils of dependency and its cycles of poverty and despair.

Without revitalizing the truest essence of the American Dream for many of the forgotten within America – those lost within the urban centers of the nation where 80% of our countrymen live…without providing hope through shrinking government and increasing opportunities and efficiencies, we are unable to take back America for all of us. That is why I conclude in telling you that our T-E-A Party now – our Taxed Enough Already movement – must also be a T-E-A Party that Touts Exceptionalism in America IF we are to usher back in the America you grew up to know and love…the America you fought for in foreign wars…the America promised to us all by a bold federal Constitution and bequeathed to us by brave countrymen alike.

A "Taxed Enough Already" movement requires that the people demand accountability from its government before they don the gauntlets to commence a revolution. A "Touting of Exceptionalism in America" invites our current politicians to reconsider their positions, even as we work to usher in a renaissance that removes their wasteful mindset from elected office. In a revolt, the energy is divisive and the warring can be destructive. In a renaissance, our passion can be peaceful, the people can be vigilant, and the power within our diversity can be embraced without slander or slight.

Our T-E-A Party – both from before today and that of now– seeks not to divide America and lock out Americans as we did through the past 2 years of leadership in Washington and the past few months of government in Springfield. We come together in a tax day revolt to bring to our state and our nation a new day of renaissance in Illinois and throughout America. Our renaissance shares a common vision for Americans, from the projects of Englewood to the mansions of Evanston. It is a vision showing us that without expansive and expensive government driving jobs from our communities to weaken employment, without government promoting social engineering programs that destroy Black families, and without government propping up self-serving bureaucrats and big-spending liberals to pamper them through ineffective and inefficient government...

...with proper government restraint, we have a chance to reclaim unity, re-embrace 360-degree accountability, and truly indeed take back America.

For those gathered in Springfield today and for those that love America as we do that could not be here with us, I implore you: yesterday was the time for you to have a Taxed Enough Already Party, but for today and beyond, we must also Tout Exceptionalism in America, stop partying, and get to work, particularly if we are to tout excellence throughout our nation and successfully reclaim the promise, the forgotten, the lost, and the best of America.

The opportunity to uplift America in all facets of society through smaller government and bigger people is upon us.

The work to be done to improve America is all around us. Our neighbors pleading for leaders are calling on us from the holler to the hills. And the obligations from our ancestors from Africa and Austria...to Ireland and Italy...are beckoning to us, simply saying:

Beloved patriots, your time is now.

Thank you for this opportunity to speak with you today. May God Bless you always. May God Bless the state of Illinois, and May God Bless the United States of America.

Lenny McAllister: 4th of July Celebration Event
2009 July 4 ("**From C to C to C**")

Hello, fellow Americans and fellow patriots. Happy 4th of July to you all.

People around the country are still calling events like today pieces of the tea party movement, an effort where citizens gather together in order to protest the direction that our nation is moving in.

However, today, I would like to move us in another way. The first two times that we came together as a group, we focused on the tea party of the equation. We abhorred higher taxes. We spoke out against bigger, wasteful government.

Although there is a time and a place to protest against the failures and inefficiencies of expensive, broken promises by a rapidly expanding federal government…

…and although there is certainly a time as North Carolinians to protest the irresponsibility behind a push to raise taxes by $1.5 billion over the next 2 years…

…today is not the day to focus on the "tea" in "tea party"…

…today is the day to focus on the "party"

July 4th is a day to celebrate the greatness of our nation, from a historical basis and from a contemporary perspective. It is a day to appreciate the beginnings that we have fostered as a nation and discuss the new beginnings that we must take on as well. It is a day to understand what was done for us by others in order to create this great nation, and it is a day to comprehend what we must do for our children and grandchildren to uphold what makes America great.

The 4th of July has been a marker for both beginnings and endings. It is the day when the conception of the United States of America was born. It is the day when one American president was born – President Calvin Coolidge – and it is a day when we lost three other presidents in passing – President James Monroe and Founding Fathers Presidents John Adams and Thomas Jefferson.

On this day in 1776, the text for our great Declaration of Independence was finalized by the Founding Fathers of America on this day, showing us the great path that we can take as a united people against oppression, tyranny, and government that holds back its citizens instead of listening to and working with its citizens. Its  verbiage is not mere words; it is the embodiment of empowerment of people and the literary light-post of liberty. They said then what we say now, that:

"We hold these truths to be self-evident, that all men are created equal, that they are endowed by their Creator with

certain unalienable Rights, that among these are Life,
Liberty and the pursuit of Happiness."

July 4th is also a day to challenge ourselves to not become
complacent, to not get caught up in a display of fireworks, cotton
candy, and Americana while not being true to our values
continuously. In the midst of the July 4th Celebration of 1852,
patriot Frederick Douglass reminded America of the adage that
would be uttered a century later by Dr. Martin Luther King, Jr:
that injustice anywhere is a threat to justice everywhere. In the
midst of celebration, Frederick Douglass reminded his audience
that there were great challenges before them, just as there are for
us today. Using Douglass' words, in order to keep our
celebration from being a sham…to keep our boasted liberty from
being an unholy license…and to keep our national greatness from
becoming a swelling vanity…we must comprehend the
challenges and champion our values continuously, not just during
our celebrations.

We are a country that is the beacon of the world for justice and
freedom. As we know, freedom is not without a price. We are
reminded of President Jefferson's words:

"The price of freedom is eternal vigilance."

It is this price that we must pay for each other's freedoms as
Americans if we are to truly relish the celebration of the 4th of
July. As our patriotic folksong says, if we are to prompt God to
shed His grace on us, we must
crown our good with the brotherhood of freedom, from sea to
shining sea.

The SEAS are before us today. They are not the 2 SEAS of the song, "America the Beautiful." They are the 3 Cs that we stand before us on the 4th of July, prompting us to take on the mantra of the Founding Fathers of this great land. It took great leaders in colonial times to forge the Mecklenburg Declaration of Independence in 1775 and the American Declaration of Independence in 1776. It will take great leaders today to secure, promote, and declare our independence today.

So, what is the 4th of July to Americans across our great land today? It is a day of small beginnings and big dreams, where the impossible for the good of justice and freedom is forever possible because of this nation and its people

It is a day to experience ours highs as a people and a day to study our lows as a nation. And to do that, we must ride the 3 Cs.

July 4th is a day to reclaim ourselves as citizens of this great nation. The "C" in citizens is the first "C" that we must take on together. We must declare our responsibility to be active in the formation of laws, aware of how our community forms around us, and vocal in our support or dissent of actions taken by the government on our behalf. We must be vocal against inefficiencies and corruption. We must be cognizant of the design that our Founding Fathers put into place for this nation so that we can embody their vision of these United States. We must be active in the administration of government so that government can stop being so administrative.

When government is administrative, justice and freedom are rationed. Rationed justice and freedom are symptomatic of the very tyranny this country was founded in 1776 in order to avoid.

We – the responsible and proud citizens here on the 4th of July – cannot tolerate this any longer.

And we are not alone in this stance. Around the world, we see the spirit of America uplifting people to be represented by rule of law, not by iron fist.

The people of Iran are standing up against the corruption of a questionable election and detestable violence by the government against courageous protesters. Some have died as martyrs but all of them live as examples of freedom, as they sadly enact President Jefferson's words when he said that:

> "The tree of liberty must be refreshed from time to time with the blood of patriots and tyrants."

The Supreme Court and Congress of Honduras are moving patriotically against its leftist president intent on superseding their constitution and imposing his will over the will of his people.

Some countries have denounced this. Our history as a nation declares every July 4th that all countries must have that same courage to prioritize intact constitutions over inconveniences and impoliteness.

I understand that one of those countries against this move is the United States as directed by Washington. Funny, how the city where this directive came from was named after a patriot that prioritized upholding a constitution of inalienable rights over the inconvenience provided by tyranny.

So, it prompts us to beg the question, in light of a dangerous backslide of Americanism in Washington:

…if the people of Iran can embody the spirit of America to push for justice…

…and if the government of Honduras can embody the spirit of America to protect their freedom…

…and as other countries around the world continue to look to the United States of America as an example of hope and prosperity…

…when are we as the American government going to stop acting like the rest of the world and go back to acting like the United States of America?

I say we start today, and to start today, it must ride the wave of the first SEA: CITIZENS.

It will take citizens taking on the second C – challenges. We must take on these challenges with consistency. Author Ambrose Bierce once opined that:

"The vote is the instrument and symbol of a freeman's power to make a fool of himself and a wreck of his country."

The 4th of July is a great opportunity to prove Mr. Bierce wrong.

Today is beginning of making the vote a 365-day investment into the lives of our neighbors and into the vision of our communities. July 4th is the portal to every November, and its spirit calls us to engage our challenges as patriots so that our love is resourceful, not vain.

American civil rights activist El-Hajj Malik El-Shabazz reflected the warnings of our forefathers, saying that

"…(we are) not to be so blinded with patriotism that (we) can't face reality. Wrong is wrong, no matter who does it or says it."

And this is true. Wrong is wrong, whether it comes from the halls of Congress, the General Assembly in Raleigh, or the hands within our communities. And as citizens, we are called to never be blinded to our challenges, whether it is by zeal for country or by apathy for history. We are called to lift our hearts in worship of God, our hands in labor for prosperity, and our voices in defense of the American way of life.

We are challenged each 4th of July to understand our Declaration of Independence and our Constitution. We are challenged to know our history, a history where we did not discriminate against those that did not hold our Judeo-Christian values…even as our Founding Fathers proudly and regularly quoted the Bible for strength and reference in building these United States.

In honor of their historical example, we should look to the example within the Holy Bible to ready us to confront and conquer our challenges.

One of my favorite passages is from the book of Ephesians, Chapter 6. It is here where the Ephesian church was told how to use the Word of God to ready the church for their spiritual challenges in the day of St. Paul. In a similar fashion, we must use the Constitution and Declaration of Independence to ready us for our challenges today.

They were told to clothe in the Word of God to stand firm against the tactics of the devil. Today, we must clothe ourselves in the Constitution to stand firm against the un-American growth of government.

They were told to gird themselves in the Word with truth, and today, we must tighten ourselves with the truth behind the formation of this great nation as found in the Constitution, binding our outreach of bureaucracy in the process.

They were told to cover their hearts with righteousness in the Word, and today, we must embrace the Constitution and Declaration of Independence, holding it near our hearts as the legal and moral compasses to do what is right as a nation.

They were told to use the Word of God as shoes for readiness to act for the gospel, and today, we must take our founding documents and use them as avenues to act, to be ready, to be educated, and to be victorious in confronting our domestic and international challenges as a nation without compromising the American Way in the process.

Paul implores them to take faith as a shield to reject all attempts to destroy what is great. The founding fathers took this faith and created the greatest country in the world. Therefore, I implore us today to take faith as we embrace the third and final C:

Commitment

Citizens cannot overcome the challenges of these adverse times without a sound commitment to our principles and our people. Our patriotism must be rooted in deference to our proud past and hard work today if we are going to secure longevity as the world's beacon of hope. We see your commitment here today, celebrating the best that America is. We have seen your commitment before, protesting the land that America threatens to become.

I ask of you today: can we count on your commitment for tomorrow as we work to secure America's longevity?

I once said in a speech that every day is Election Day…but for this to be true in its most efficient, most prosperous, and most patriotic way possible…

…every day, starting today, must be the 4th of July.

Every day must have our commitment to do more with smaller government and a bigger personal responsibility to uphold what is right, for upholding what is right is truly American.

Every day must have our commitment to educate our neighbors on the merits of our past with a sense of respect in disagreement, honor in our commonality, and vision for how we can make things better.

Every day must have our commitment to be courageous when it is unpopular and virtuous when it is inconvenient.

Every day must have our commitment to look back to 1776 to remember what America is supposed to be in 2009, so that we look to our Founding Fathers for greatness and not to our peers for mediocrity.

Every day must have our commitment to be free and unique, not encumbered and common.

In an era of great challenges from aboard, President John F. Kennedy said simply:

> "Ask not what your country can do for you - ask what you can do for your country."

In this era of great challenges from aboard as well as within, it is time for our commitment to ask all Americans:

> "Ask not what un-American growth of big government can build for your life – ask what the work of your hands, the commitment to your Constitution, and the patriotism of the American Way can build for a greater America."

> "Ask not how to empower your government to legislate an economy – ask how to empower people to institute longevity and prosperity."

> "Ask not the meaning of the 4th of July, 1776 – ask what the 4th of July means each and every day in 2009 and beyond."

The 4th is a day of small beginnings and the American Dream, where the impossible for the good of justice and freedom is forever possible because of the greatness of this nation and its people.

Today is our small beginning. It is time to go from SEA to shining SEA to fulfill our American Dream.

Thank you for this opportunity. God Bless this great state of North Carolina and God Bless the United States of America.

Lenny McAllister: Take Back Our State Tea Party
2009 June 3 ("**Wall**")

Hello, fellow North Carolinians and fellow Americans. Thank you for having me today here in our state's capital. Thank you for being involved and staying involved.

Before I continue, I want to clarify why I am here today and, perhaps, why you are here as well.

People believe that we are here to protest taxes. However, paying a tax is much like using thumb tacks. If they are used correctly, they hold things up without much notice from anyone. They are barely seen but plenty useful. If you use them improperly, they can be a terrible annoyance, pulling holes in structures unnecessarily and even pricking yourself in the finger and

drawing a little blood.

With the proposal of raising taxes by over $1 billion over the course of the next 2 fiscal years, we are not just talking about taxes – or even thumb tacks. We are talking about bricks.

Like thumb tacks, bricks can be very helpful if used the right way.

Bricks can be used to pay down the foundation of a better tomorrow for North Carolina. If used properly, they can be used to build roads where they are needed, schools where students must learn, and structures where adults can work and live. Like taxes, if the resource is spent properly, our bricks can build structures that support prosperity.

That is, if it is spent correctly…if the premise is sound.

However, that is not what we find today in Raleigh or throughout North Carolina. That is why we are here today.

With a tax rate among the upper echelons of the country, we continue to find commerce inadequacies on our roads. Despite high taxes and an education lottery, we continue to see our children fail in schools at embarrassing rates. With the second highest corporate tax rate in the South, we risk seeing people come to North Carolina to live while jobs leave North Carolina for greener pastures to the south of us, to the west of us, and to the north of us.

Our money bricks are not building legacy. They threaten it.

They create bureaucracy that continues to threaten the personal freedoms of the people. Building out government eventually means building up barriers that block North Carolinians from creating jobs, creating avenues for better education, and creating avenues for assisting others. Building up structures without building in sensibility with how we spend only leads to a government that silences the sweet music of a prosperous people.

To have such a high tax rate and look to raise it when North Carolinians are suffering is impractical.

To have such a high corporate tax rate while having the collective poor condition of our schools and our students' performances is immoral.

To continue to look to spend our way out of a recession when we have seen the failures of the Obama Administration as they spent their way to bankruptcy court with GM and Chrysler and performance bonuses for AIG and others…

…that is inexcusable.

These bricks…these tax dollars…are not being used to build efficiently in North Carolina. Instead, they continuously erect a wall that divide the people of North Carolina from a higher influx of jobs. This wall separates North Carolinians from a higher quality of education for their children by continuously dumping into a school structure without fixing the hole through which our money…and North Carolina's children…continue to fall through. This wall continues to blockade our citizens from saving for legacy, building for the future, and passing on to our loved ones our vision and hard work from our toils.

Each excessive tax that further inhibits the people of North Carolina to create more jobs, create better educated communities, and create an American dream for each of their families is a brick in the ever-increasing wall blocking us from what this great state should be for us and for America.

Can you see the wall rising? I can.

And each attempt to raise taxes both without a clear vision of personal financial strength and direction for its citizens and without tangible results is a ruse to cement the presence of big government in the lives of businesses and residents of North Carolina. This effort – this wall - insulates the government's decisions from the voice of the people. It also separates a representative government from the will of the people as well.

This wall continues to be an expensive barrier between time-tested values and practices to bring prosperity to more North Carolinians. With each brick laid by the plans to increase taxes, we are not building a path to more personal prosperity; we are building a wall blocking our way to a Glory Road for us all.

This wall builds jails without creating ways to keep children from becoming criminals through sound education. This wall inhibits business growth but wants employers and employees to pay more taxes.

This wall already threatens to keep more North Carolinians behind in the 21st Century, a reality we cannot afford. We need more talent creating, more people working, and more people contributing in making the Great State of North Carolina a better place to work and live.

This wall of high taxes is high enough.

This wall separating us from the prosperity that we can have is high enough.

This wall of inefficient spending is too high and it is blocking our government from hearing the will of the people.

So, although America and North Carolina are moving in a dangerous direction, I am still not President Reagan.

But when it comes to the wall of inefficient spending…

…and when it comes to the wall of competition-limiting taxation…and when it comes to the wall blocking us from more jobs and better lives…

I must paraphrase the 40th president in our quest to see North Carolina achieve its fullest potential.

So I say respectfully: Madame Governor – tear down this wall!

Thank you for this opportunity. God Bless this great state of North Carolina and God Bless the United States of America.

Lenny McAllister: 2010 July 26 (Republican Party of Lee County / Speaker Series) (Ernest and Ruby McSwain Agriculture Center, 2420 Tramway Road, Sanford, NC). ("**Conviction for the 3 Rs during Today's Teachable Moment**")

Good evening, everyone. I hope that you are having a great week so far.

Before I begin with my prepared remarks, I want to take this moment to thank a few people for their continued support as I make another trip out to this wonderful part of the Tar Heel State. First, let me say thank you to Ms. Linda Shook for inviting me to participate as the inaugural speaker for the Republican Party of Lee County's Speaker Series. It is an honor to be the first one selected to come out and speak to the fine folks out there – not just the members of my political party, but also those North Carolinians that made the trip out here this evening to engage themselves in another conversation that, God willing, will allow us to move past the obstacles before us to a more prosperous and more peaceful way of life for us all. Thank you, Linda, for allowing me to be the first, but I am certain that I will not be the last speaker in this series.

I also want to say thank you to a few other friends before I continue.

Let me say thank you to Ms. Ginger Ballard. She invited my family and me out here for me to speak a few months ago out in this area. My infant son Neilan and my wife Lannie had a good time out here, primarily because they ate while I spoke. However, there is nothing like North Carolina hospitality being extended to my family while I am working with folks to discuss the troubles before our state and nation today. Thank you, Ginger, for that opportunity.

I also want to extend a thank you publicly to my friend Michael Martz who was willing to drive me out here this evening when my personal transportation proved unreliable right now. Mr. Martz has been a good friend to my family for 10 years now. He has witnessed the challenges, triumphs, and compromises that I have had to undergo while attempting to – as I once repeated regularly on Fox Charlotte during my editorials – "bring politics back to the people." Folks, there are those out there that do *not* want politics to be put back in the hands of people like you and me…like Mr. Martz and Ms. Shook. I can assure you – Michael Martz has witnessed it first hand in my life, but he understands – just as many other friends and loved ones that support me understand – that what we are embarking upon today is a movement for future generations, so the inconvenience and discomfort in the long term is worthwhile. If you will, please give him a round of applause for his willingness to sacrifice today so that I can be here with you this evening.

And, of course, I want to thank God for this moment before you today and thank God for my wife and best friend on earth. She gives her regrets for not being able to attend this evening. I tell you, though, that she is committed to turning around this ship that we are in together – for the sake of our family and for the sake of future Americans that will need our courage today in order to provide a chance for American continuity tomorrow. I just want to take a moment before I begin to thank her for her support of me now and always.

Now, we have heard from the White House this week that we are living amongst a "teachable moment" – on race, as far as they are concerned. However, I think that if we look into the depths of the challenges that our nation is facing today, this presidential term – and perhaps, even, the term before it – has been one collective "teachable moment" for our nation. If we are going to maximize the lessons before us and reshape the greatest nation on earth, it behooves us to take advantage of this moment and apply the basics at our disposal in order to take hold over the complexities of over-regulation within the nation, over-emotionalism between Americans, and under communication amongst the citizens and our governments that have stymied growth in our nation, jobs in our communities, and confidence in our leaders.

When we talk about academics in America today, we hear about how our schools are enough emphasizing the 3 Rs like educators used to do in days long gone. Therefore, I decided to make the theme of my remarks to you today, "Our Conviction for the 3 Rs during Today's Teachable Moment." As we may remember, the 3 Rs aren't really Rs at all, but they were – and still are – considered the basic tenets of education that our children need to leverage and master in order to hold the keys of their future – and America's future prosperity – in their hands. Those principles – writing, arithmetic, and reading – are not planks in a forgone platform of education that made sense in the one-room schoolhouses from decades ago. Just the same, these principles are not just the ingredients of a catchy slogan for education. These principles – the 3 Rs – are keys to our future as Americans as well. These are tenets that I urge you to hang onto today – as Republicans, as conservatives, as Tea Party patriots, and as Americans of all creeds and backgrounds. The 3 Rs will lead us in action for a better America or we will ignore them as we continue down a path of mediocrity, of debt, and of national despair and instability.

Out of the 3 Rs, let's start with writing – the Rs that is actually a W.

If we are going to get the "W" that we need in this battle against the socialization of America…if we are going to get the "W" – the WIN – that we need in this battle against the notion of American exceptionalism…we must ensure that we are picking up the pen of history and writing our names in the history books – for change, for improvements, for peace, and for the unimaginable successes that our forefathers dared to pursue in 1776, in 1860, in 1941, and during the 1950s and 1960s. Our national belief that America can be #1 in education, in economics, in diplomacy and, if necessary, in military might is under attack – that notion of exceptionalism is part of the national fabric that makes America the example for the free world and the hope of legal immigrants for decades as a land of opportunity, of freedom, of justice, and of accomplishing dreams. That notion is under attack from career politicians and big government leaders that drive our communities into the ground with legislative pride in the place of representative government. It is our duty today to act – just as it was for the founders of this nation and the authors of the Declaration of Independence and our national Constitution to act. It is our duty to act through picking up our pens today…just as we are called as Christians to pick up our crosses daily….we must pick up the obligations of involvement in our government, in our elections, and in the conversations that impact our lives and write a better course of action for our communities.

We have a historical obligation to the soldiers that died on the battlefields across the nation to pick up the pen of history today just as they courageously picked up swords and guns in order to defend our freedom – both now in the Middle East as well as before these current times. And, know this: it does take courage to pick up the pen of history each day to write a better course for our nation. Now, why is that? Because writing – a new direction, a better course of action – it takes forward thought. Writing takes courage to act in faith for what you want to create instead of waiting for others to dictate to you. Writing involves a person's creativity –a freedom that cannot be contained by circumstance but, rather, is similar to the God-ordained protected by the Constitution. On the other hand, without picking up our collective pen to write a better history for our nation, we merely allow big government, big bureaucracy, and big brother opposition to dictate life to us. Dictation of life limits personal freedoms and discourages creativity. Dictation restricts expansion. It strangles growth. It takes the citizen out of the process of making her or his country. If writing incorporates personal liberty, dictation reflects personal oppression.

We are seeing throughout America a need for new writing, not more dictation, if we are going to embrace personal liberties for all. And what does writing a new history for the future of America entail? It involves a re-education of the nation through the grassroots involvement that tea party activists, online conversations, and everyday talks with neighbors represents. America is the greatest nation with the greatest level of freedoms, creativity, and diversity that the world has ever known. It is on us to take the powerful pen those attributes provide for us in order to write a new way of dealing with 21st century problems. It is on us to take this challenge to write a new course of action to dictate to government how our challenges will be engaged and how people will be empowered through citizen-centric solutions. Authors in life take the pen of history – with their activism, with their common concern for our nation, and with a vision to create something better – to make a positive difference in the midst of chaos, miscommunication, and mishaps. American political and social activism in the 21st century must be full of authors – those willing to write and create a better America. We must embrace the first R – writing – if we are going to gain a W – a win – in our current battle against the timeless struggle of human freedom, dignity, and prosperity incorporated in the standard we hold dear as the American Way of Life.

Without activist authors – those willing to engage the system and our political and societal problems today in order to correct it – we will lose out on the 2 R – arithmetic. Simply put, without those willing to make history as citizen leaders, the math just won't add up in America. Now, granted, I know that this is also another one of those "Rs" that isn't really an R. However, it is a tenet to our political activism and involvement today that we must consider a daily requirement – something that operates outsides of the Rs or D; (that is, Republicans and Democrats.) Never mind the national debt that continues to mount up without sensible fiscal responsibility in Raleigh or in Washington, DC. For a moment, let's try to ignore the disabling unemployment throughout North Carolina or the nearly 10% national figure for the jobless, including numbers twice as high for young people trying to make their futures in the midst of such a tough contemporary time. If we are not able to equate our messages of smaller government, better business opportunities, freer school choices for parents, and less restrictive bureaucracy for our citizens, we will lose America as the end result will not add up to voters that understand why this current direction leads to a looming future for us all. The math of piling up trillions of dollars in debt on expansive programs that limit freedom, erode quality, and expand government bureaucracy does not add up in a time when more Americans need small business owners to hire and when more Americans need more money in their pockets to weather this crucial storm. The math does not add up in this nation when Wall Street continues to make gains under the bailout and stimulus plans of the past two presidents while Main Street continues to lose jobs to a point where people stop looking for work.

If the authors of America are going to write a better course of action for us all, where must this all add to a better result? My friends, in the American equation of government, there was always intended to be a balance between the citizens within this republican form of government and the representatives that were sent to town halls, state capitols, and Washington DC to serve those people. That is what the writers of the Constitution intended. Just the same time, we now need to ensure the balance of the America equation of government once again. We need more activism on the citizen side of the ledger, not more authors of bureaucracy and over-regulation on the big government side of the equation. To re-balance America, we need numbers. We need more people that love America and love the promise of this nation more than we love being right in the demagoguery of pop politics or media tussles that use our problems as a nation as the reality-television props for ratings, not resolutions. We need more people that are willing to take on the mantra of "smaller government, bigger people," so that as we cut wasteful programs that are bankrupting our nation morally, ethically, and monetarily, we re-expand the role of everyday Americans into their proper roles of everyday superheroes, administrators of their communities through the common fabric of Americanism that allows us to see and embrace diversity while clinging to the national and shared thread that makes us one nation, under God, and truly indivisible despite the tough times we are in. We need more people that embrace our past, learn from our mistakes, believe in our Constitution, and have faith that we will prosper as the world's leader – its shining city on a hill. In order to make the math add up for empowering leadership in this time of crisis, we need to math up: add to the number of activist American authors of a better history without merely becoming a number to be dictated to by the powers that be. It is time for us to be that power.

Our third R is, well, actually a R: it's reading. However, it's more than just reading. In our troubled times and in our season of national discord, it is more than just reading the great documents within our history and moving forward from there. It is more than just reading the Constitution and re-embracing the true definitions of the federal government, not reading into the self-prescribed notions of big government as we have seen over the past several decades. It is more than just reading the great speeches from American leaders such as Frederick Douglass, Martin Luther King, John F. Kennedy, Ronald Reagan, and others in order to remember what we are as a nation – and who we have excelled in becoming past our previous social, geopolitical, and fiscal challenges. It is about reading the moment. It is about reading into the nuances of our contemporary times and understanding what our call to history should entail. It is about reading over the lessons of the past and reading the hearts of our fellow Americans in order to find the best methods to write a new course for our nation and add to the numbers of those required to make the positive changes back towards our republican form of government as constituted by the founding fathers of these United States. Without a sense of "reading the tea leaves," if you will, what good would it do to claim the pen of history before us? What good would it do for us to add to the numbers of Americans marching in the streets today? Without reading through the wisdom of the past and the honor that our ancestors oblige us to – Americans of all shades and creeds that made this nation through struggles and strife – what good does it do us to act? Therefore, we must make sure that while we are actively picking up the pen of history in order to creatively draft an American way of life that more Americans can enjoy…and while we make sure that we constructively add to the numbers of voices being heard throughout a land of frustrated citizens that demand change that equates to more than just catchy campaign slogans, bumper stickers, and nightly quips in the news cycle…while we are doing the necessary writing and doing the needed arithmetic for improving our nation, we must make sure that we are reading both the lessons of our past and the sign of the times correctly.

Without applying the 3 Rs of academics to our education of improving e political and social dynamics of contemporary America, we are left fighting a dynamic that we are currently facing. Without proper application today, the 3 Rs – writing, arithmetic, and reading – W, A, R – can lead us to R – A – W – raw, as in the raw sensitivity that most of us as Americans are feeling today over issues including race, illegal immigration, the mid-term elections, and the proficiency – or misgivings – of the Obama Administration. Without proper application of our 3 Rs, the 3 Rs – writing, arithmetic, and reading – W, A, R - we will continue our national experience with the internal war that we are undergoing, a battle where ideals are weapons to fight fellow citizens, not pathways to lead us all to a better America. Without the courage to create, the numbers to act, and the wisdom to seize the moment, we will be a nation that is dictated to by an out-of-control government, inflating numbers and debt past the point of return, ignorant of our past greatness or current potential to achieve even more as a beacon of good in our land and throughout the world.

So, as Tea Party patriots, as Republicans, as author-activists writing a new history, and as Americans looking to build a better way for us all – we have to ask: what is the best application of the 3 Rs?

I tell you today: it comes from our conviction for the 3 relevant Rs that we have discovered through the teachable moment over the past few weeks – and, in fact, over the past 18 months in our nation.

One teachable R within our nation today must be about race. This is a lesson for all of us, from Tea Party patriots to the newest member of the NAACP. In today's time…with today's fears and with our contemporary realities of diversity, racial disparities, racial harmony, and perhaps even overlooked racial segregation, we must have the courage to honor the struggle of the past with an honest, direct, and healing 21st century discussion on race in America. This conversation – if we are to be successful – must be authored by the people of America, not dictated to by the media or the fear-mongers amongst us. We must define the racial challenges of today in today's terms. For example, not all Tea Party activists…and, in my experience, the vast majority of them are God-fearing Americans that love all people as children of God and brethren in Christ. If we are going to heal past the recent wounds from racial realities today, we must not prejudge a movement of loving Americans on the foolery of a select few in the media. Just the same, as tea party patriots, we must not be afraid to embrace the melting pot nature of our nation, knowing that our diversity has historically yielded our strength, our creativity, our innovation, and our moxie to be leaders throughout the world in culture, in science, in education, and in peace-making initiatives for decades. That same diversity has also afforded us situations where inequalities do exist and, in fact, there are vastly different American experiences for those within our nation based on demographics. If we as conservatives are not willing to speak directly to the realities that the disadvantaged among us experience regularly, how can we eliminate the big government trap that many were reeled into at the risk of losing their family dynamic, jeopardizing their personal liberties, and perpetuating a cycle of poverty and mistrust for whom they deem "outsiders?" As authors of a better America, I call on us today to create a new path for the United States – one where our courage to embrace the contemporary conversations designed to separate us become the dialogue that unites us through our diversity and binds us with the common bond of being American. We must read the signs before us. We must add to the numbers that reach out around us. We must author a better way that what we have seen in our midst over the recent times.

For proper application, the second R we must take on is redemption.

The beauty of the republican form of government is its redemptive qualities if the citizenry takes on its obligations to debate, to discuss, and to dive into the knowledge of the workings of government that are available in a free society. Tea Party patriots are taking on this task today, and I urge those that may not agree with the tea party politics to look at the tea party example and become experts on your homeland. Do not surrender the greatness of America through the complacency of contemporary expectations. The current times expect you to fight to watch Jersey Shore on MTV, but the historic times we live in oblige us to fight from shore to shore – from sea to shining sea – to sure up the flaws that we have taken on. It is more than just about our government officials messing up, my fellow Americans. It is also about us not taking redemptive measures with our votes each November to heal the nation. It is also about us not taking redemptive measures to quell ignorance and prejudice before it hits the national spotlight. It is also about us not taking on the issues of imbalanced families in America, the secular movement against the presence of proper and redemptive religion in the public forum, and the growing disrespect for women, for our seniors, and for the common man in our society today. However, the beauty of the Great Experiment known as the United States of America is that we control the math that equates success and prosperity in our country. We are capable in our times…because we are called by our history…to redeem the flaws of recent past with an inspired leadership in today's time, a leadership forged by voters and activists, by taxpayers and the unemployed, by young and the old alike – as redeemed equals under the law in a nation that can prove once again to be indivisible. If we are to remain a great nation…if we are to be a great leader in the 21st century for our children and grandchildren…we must be determined to be a redeemed citizenry eager and willing to pen a new path with the constructs of our republican government that allows the people to save themselves from the tyranny of their government should it grow past its proper role in everyday life.

If we can take on race in a way that the White House, the media, and other leaders will not…and if we are willing to be redeemable through our Constitutional form of government, we will be able to bring about the third R we need today: revolution.

This is not a revolution of guns and muskets as it was in the 1770s. It is not a revolution of police guns and protests as it was in the 1950s and 1960s. This revolution, however, involves the same primary aspect that we as a nation leveraged in those instances. It takes people.

A revolution takes more than just people, folks. Writers and authors of history are not people. The masses of activists bringing change are not just numbers. The wise leadership that read the winds of change does not just peruse the times. In America, these people are visionaries. These people are dreamers. These people are workers. These people are lovers of life and defenders of those they disagree with. They debate with vigor and discuss issues with devotion to a common Constitution. They revolt against any dysfunction that impedes the Will of God in one's daily life or free will given by God through the action of government. The revolution we need today is more than just about increasing taxation; it is about understanding that increased taxation takes financial resources from those that have while continuing to limit the options of those that do not have through increased government. The revolution we need today is more than just about government amnesty for illegal immigration or government-run healthcare; it is about understanding that if government can shift the laws of right and wrong with unethical, back-room deals or sidestepping current immigration laws, there is nothing to stop government from impeding the Constitutional rights of American citizens with its next steps. The revolution we need today is more than just about winning an election in 2010 or gaining control in 2012; it is about knowing that the time is now to remove the purse-strings of government and the reins of power in this nation from the select few chosen to represent America and put them back into the hands of the people that make America run every single day. This revolution must be about understanding that Sanford stagnates with taxes and limited growth if government holds back inner city Charlotte with continued big bureaucracy. This revolution writes a better course for America so that the disadvantaged feels included in our journey, the African-American hears the message of the Tea Party without feeling prejudice, and the rural citizen in the Great Plains works with the young professional in New York City to bolster the American Way of Life – a lifestyle where liberty means more than wealth and rights mean more than being wrong or right.

My fellow Americans, if we are brave enough to conquer the 3 Rs standing before us today – Race, Redemption, and Revolution – while using the 3 Rs of today's political education – writing a better history, arithmetic to add to the right-minded activism swelling in American, and reading the hearts and minds of men and women focused on a better nation for us all – we will be victorious over the threats both internal and external that threatened to weaken the United States from a world leader to a world laggard. I believe in American exceptionalism, but in order to preserve it and improve it, we must apply it to the 3 Rs – the challenges of today with the tools from our past.

Our hearts are in the right place, but now it is time for our hands to be in the right place: holding the pen of history and writing about our courage to take back Americanism. Our presence must be found in the right place: standing with a nation of millions to honestly address our political and social challenges to heal and grow our nation. Our focus must be found to be forthright: with an ability to learn the lessons of today, lead with the inspiration of yesterday, and light a stable and prosperous path for the leaders of tomorrow.

So in closing, I thank you once again for allowing me to be here this evening.

Thank you for this opportunity to speak with you today. God Bless you all and God Bless the United States of America.

Lenny McAllister: Albany, GA / SWGA Patriots
2010 April 17 ("**Taking Back America, Taking Back Americanism**")

Good morning, Albany Tea Party Patriots!

Thank you for the opportunity to come down to Albany to speak and share time with the Southwest Georgia Patriots, the reflection of the best of America highlighted in this corner of the state.

I thank you on behalf of my lovely wife Lannie and my baby son Neilan. Thank you for inviting us down here. Further, I want to take this moment to say thank you to Ms. Donna Driskell and Ms. Vivian Stern for extending such a warm embrace to my family and me during our time here. And for the other hosts and hostesses that have been kind-hearted and thoughtful during our visit – thank you. You have made a powerful impression on us, and we thank you for your kindness.

We have come to learn in our short visit to your lovely town that this is a great place to have a good conversation with a great glass of tea. Yet, there is one thing better than that during these historic times in our nation – and that is hearing the sound of involved and educated citizens that understand the need to have a respectful, patriotic, and powerful tea party.

And it is with that power that we come together to confront the challenges that our nation faces collectively. It is with that recognized power of the people that we gather peacefully and respectfully today, asking all Americans to debate us, to engage us, to listen to us and to build a better America with us. We come humbly together to lead America back to its path of achieving better days without bigger government. We come humbly together today to guide America back to prosperous times without a disruption to the peace in the streets. We gather together in the spirit of the melting pot of America, not under the guise of hatred, racism, and fear-mongering.

So, if you think that we – the Tea Party Patriots here in southwest Georgia or throughout the nation – if you think that we are full of hate or misguided in our efforts…we invite you and, in fact, we implore you: stay and listen to us. We ask you to engage us. We ask you to debate us at the coffee shop and in the corner shop. We ask you to come in common love for America to embrace the commonality we share as Americans. We ask you today: let's build the bridge between our experiences because they are the experiences – when combined – that make up the American experience that allows us to be the best and the brightest in the world. We come to you today offering a better way for all of our families. We come together today offering a new partnership between young and old, Black and White, rich and poor – because we know full-heartedly that our collective love for the United States and our constitutional reliance on the American Dream for all of us can lead America to better days. Together, we can lead the United States back to being a force that is respected by our allies, feared by terrorists, and honored by the honorable throughout 4 corners of Georgia and undo the 4 corners of the world.

Tea Party Patriots…fellow Americans…it is time to be historic. Never before in the annals of our nation have we been up against so many walls at one time. It will only be through our collective efforts will we be able to overcome.

Last year at this time, there was a loud cry coming from all parts of the nation to highlight protests that said that they were "taxed enough already" – T E A, as in the TEA Party. Today, we are called to respond to the continued extreme leftism coming from Washington with more than protests, but with a movement. Protests are short-lived and are only prolonged actions to test the patience of the people. However, movements take us to a better place and time as a nation. Movements advance the thinking and involvement of a people. Movements take us to another level. Therefore, I am asking us to stop being a T-E-A Party group of protests. It is time to be historic and become a T-B-A Movement – a movement that does not rest until we Take Back America.

Before I continue, let me explain what we mean when I say Take Back America.

As the citizen leaders of a new movement, we understand that within leadership, there is an obligation to lead with honor, balance, and respect. With these qualities in tow, we must work to take back our nation with a sense of honor among fellow Americans, a return to proper balance between government's role and her citizens' personal freedom, and a resounding and unquestioned respect for our philosophical and political adversaries within our borders. Therefore, our efforts to take back America can never be focused on skin color, gender, or socioeconomic differences. To take the American goodness of the Tea Party movement – or the T-B-A Movement – and hi-jack it to promote hatred or racism is purely un-American. Not only is this hi-jacking un-American, it is also unacceptable, particularly at a time when we must respectfully reject other unacceptable actions within America.

I say that we cannot spend our patriotic time refuting the ignorant objections to President Obama based on race alone when we have too much work to do to raise objections to Obamacare, a dangerous health care package that risks bankrupting many Americans with its expansive taxes while limiting personal freedoms for all Americans with its restrictions and legislative oversight from Washington, DC.

We cannot spend time objecting to President Obama as the first Black commander-in-chief when too many of our allies are objecting to his vision of global balance and international affairs – just as our enemies such as North Korea and Iran are feeling too cozy in their ability to scoff at our demands for maintaining nuclear peace throughout the world.

The patriots that stand with me understand that it is not about the White House going black – it is about getting the United States economy and ledger line back into the black…before we drown in red as a nation.

Taking Back America is taking back YOUR America – regardless of race, creed, gender, or other delineation within the melting pot of our great nation. Take Back America is honoring

YOUR history – a history where scientists came from historically Black universities and colleges as well as Harvard University and Davidson College…a history where Nobel Prizes were collected by Jewish immigrants and Black southern preachers alike. Taking Back America is saying that we will take a stand against the big-government movement that threatens to permanently weaken our country – even as we take a stand against the hatred and social toxicity coming from a fringe element that threatens to de-legitimize Tea Partiers and their collective cause throughout the land.

When we mention our new movement – the T-B-A Movement to Take Back America – we say this with the mindset of taking America's politicians back to a place where the American people are trusted in this nation as a citizenry of leaders to bolster our economy, have a sense of stability in our communities, and instill a new sense of American pride. We are taking America away from the stranglehold of bureaucrats in far-away board rooms and legislature halls that make decisions for everyday Americans – the good people from Albany, Georgia to Anaheim, California and points in between…good people that they refuse to listen to and have ignored their accountability to for far too long.

When we mention "taking back America", we are reclaiming the pursuit of happiness that the authors of the Declaration of Independence sought for us to have today, just as we enjoy the freedom of speech and assembly that we enjoy at this very moment.

When we mention taking back America, we believe in giving an America to our children and grandchildren that is not owned by the Chinese or other nations because of our unchecked and irresponsible spending habits from the past 2 presidential administrations. We refuse to allow these habits to go unchecked anymore. No sir – no ma'am: never again.

From town hall forums to city council meetings to voting booths, we will promote personal accountability and legislative accountability, bringing about a symbiotic relationship between citizens and their representative government that can end the cycle of career politicians that win 90% of the elections each time by pleasing only 20% of their constituents.

When we take back America, we mean that we will take back our nation from special interests groups and, in fact, BECOME the special interest group that matters most – everyday, energetic, and engaged American citizens.

And when we mention taking back America, we believe in a nation that honors people over government. We believe in a country that supports its citizens over the concerns of the global community. We believe in a network of leaders that demand humble, servant leadership from their elected officials immediately under the threat of kicking any ungrateful politicians out of office in November.

The movement that we start today – the T.B.A. Movement – prompts us to have the courage to envision a better America even during these dark days. This movement that we are called by our forefathers to start today asks us to love each other enough to act, care about each other enough to debate, and respect our forefathers enough to tough it out until we are once again victorious.

As they said starting in 2009: when the going gets tough, the tough....drink tea!

Yet, to find our way for a better America, patriots, we must have vision. And to have the proper vision for America, we must be able to SEA – S.E.A.

For, unlike many in Washington – from the White House to the Speaker of the House – for us to get America back on track, we must be able to SEA – Support Exceptionalism in America.

Our humble pride in the United States of America must once again prompt us to be the shining city on a hill, not be an apologetic figure in the world because of our hard work, our generosity around the world, and our desire to be the leader in the world as a provider of good, a beacon of freedom, and a force to be reckoned with economically, educationally, and – if need be - militarily.

S-E-A – (Support Exceptionalism for America)

 We must be able to SEA – that America is a force of good in the world …that it is better for America's military might to stay intact, not acquiesce to the popular yet misguided whims of other nations to reduce our nuclear arsenal, even as the president admits that the nuclear threat globally is going up, not going down.

127

We must be able to SEA that America will never regain its status as the economic superpower in the world if elitism from the nation's capital dictates how grassroots Americans will raise their children, educate their students, create their jobs, and live their lives. We must be exceptional in our ability to provide self-determination once again throughout America – where race, creed, socioeconomic background, or previous obstacles in life are not enough to stop the American Dream from being an everyday reality in the lives of more Americans regardless of their lot in life.

We must be exceptional in honoring the farmers of America the same way we respect the financial directors of Fortune 500 companies. Central planning from Washington and elitism in the halls of Congress will never restore American wealth or honor. American exceptionalism never came from American government workers or American politicians. It came from the American form of government that understood that American power in all forms comes directly from the American people. Our vision for the future must see that leading a new America prompts us to take back America to a time where respect for our Constitution was high, our constitution of self and our abilities were stronger, and our willingness to construct a socialist model of spending did not exist.

We must go back to a principle where Americans build America instead of politicians dictating to America. We build our dreams because of less government intrusion, more personal interaction, and more American ingenuity. We must bring America back to a place where getting our hands dirty for all of the right reasons is a sign of knowing that we are on the right path for better days ahead.

Fellow patriots, we are called today to begin the T-B-A Movement, but we cannot begin to Take Back America if we cannot see – S.E.A. – what that new America must look like.

If we truly Support Exceptionalism in America once again, it will take smaller government, bigger people.

If we are willing to take government back to its proper place in our lives, we must be willing to assume the bigger role of people to understand how our laws affect our lives, how our local economies make our communities viable, and how our humble leadership in everyday examples both big and small take us to the next level of expanding prosperity for more Americans in the 21st century.

If we are willing to take government back to its proper place in our lives, we must have the vision to SEA American Exceptionalism in our ghettos and our working class neighborhoods. We must see future leaders in the eyes of our children suffering there. We must see future businessmen and congresswomen in their destinies as we see them grow from childhood to adulthood. And we must encourage them to see it in themselves – for their benefit as Americans and for our benefit to have co-contributors to the American Dream for us all. When we use this vision to Support Exceptionalism in America with the most challenged among us today, we must look to invest our time and patriotism as well in order to strengthen our nation not with money and bureaucracy, but with humble pride and true hope.

I am calling on all of us today to use the same passion that we use to protest the taxation and spending from Washington – and double it to foster the seeds for innovative scientists, successful business leaders, caring teachers, stable parents, and ethical politicians that we need to replant the American Dream in the futile ground of our ready nation.

We cannot compete in the global economy with more taxation, job-killing legislation, and restrictive regulation. We can win in the global economy once again if we get government out of the way as we create more jobs, increase the educational achievements of our children, and stabilize our communities with self-accountable and community-accountable goals, not edicts from almighty Washington.

My beloved countrymen and countrywomen, we can protest the spending in Washington alone – or we can focus on the movement that we need to restore American values in government, restore America's definition of government, and remind American politicians of the proper role of government. My fellow patriots, we can merely complain about growing entitlements and earmarks from Washington or we can begin to eliminate the conditions that create entitlements and earmarks – even as we also begin to eliminate the politicians pushing this expansive spending from the roll call of Congress starting in 2010.

Good people, this movement stopped being just about taxes the moment our leaders in Washington stopped caring about the Constitution. Fellow Americans, this movement stopped being just about spending the moment career politicians on both sides of the aisle continued betraying the American trust with their viewpoints on America's standing in the world and their focus on their selfish gains, not our demands as an electorate. This stopped being just about money when leaders decided to focus more on race and hatred than on issues, deception, and lack of transparency from the White House and from Congressional leadership. This stopped being just about the deficit when lawmakers began cutting deals with the Louisiana Purchase, the Cornhusker Kickback, and Gator-aid in order to pass comprehensive and expensive legislation over the objections of the American people.

Therefore, you are called to be historic, honorable, passionate, powerful, persistent, and poised to take back America as we collective walk together in our pursuit of a more perfect Union.

Americans, you are called by your forefathers to be proud to extol the values of your nation. You are required by the blood of Black men, White men, Asian-Americans, and Latino-Americans that was shed for the freedom that you enjoy to protect the America that you have today – one that is threatened by an overreach of government by a group of misguided lawmakers. It is demanded of us to be historic as we confront some of the greatest challenges to the United States in the history of our nation – and we are obligated to do so with a sense of honor, of determination, and of perseverance, even as others misunderstand us, slander us, and malign us. Those obstacles are not enough to stop the progress of our movement.

The world called Frederick Douglass a slave. President Abraham Lincoln called him the man whose opinion he respected the most in the world.

The world once considered racial harmony an impossible dream. The world today calls it a bridge traveled by many successfully that welcomes the rest of us to walk its breezeway to unity.

The world once called the United States of America the gateway to freedom, the land of prosperity, and the example for others to follow. The historic call to us now calls us to ignore the temptation to lull us into apathy, the distractions to annoy us and castigate us into frustration, and the slogans to sidestep what is important to us and our descendents.

Fellow Americans – when it comes to the high levels of spending, expansive role of government, and increased actions to separate us as a nation – it is time to stop drinking the Kool-Aid.

When it comes to listening to how to lead a nation of citizens involved in educated, small-government leadership, it is time to dip into the TEA.

When it comes to reclaim the best that America can be, we must have the vision to SEA – Support Exceptionalism once again for America – both here and throughout the world.

Let's do this together, fellow Americans, for it's the only way for us to B.E.A. = Beautiful Everyday Americans.

Thank you, Albany, for this opportunity to speak to you today. God Bless you patriots, God Bless our efforts to unite our nation in prosperity and justice, and God Bless the United States of America.

Lenny McAllister: <u>Americans for Prosperity (July 21 2012):</u>
<u>Fearing American Competition, Failing in Applying American</u>
<u>Capitalism, and Falling Short as Free-Market Advocates – Yet</u>
<u>Able to Fight for Change to Restrengthen America</u>

Good afternoon, folks. God Bless you and thank you very much for allowing me to have a few minutes to speak to you this afternoon and deliver some prepared remarks.

Before I begin, I want to make sure that I once again thank my good friend Linda Ragsdale and the wonderful conservatives working hard on our collective behalf as part of the Americans for Prosperity team. Thank you folks for your efforts in putting this event together this weekend and for putting our philosophical compatriots in position to be more effective in 2012 and beyond.

As well, before I go into my remarks, I also want to make sure that I thank all of you here today for your collective efforts as well. You are here today because you care about our collective future, because you are involved in the political battles that shape our collective prospects and potential, and because you are thoroughly engaged in the political developments of the day and their nuisances.

In essence, you get into the weeds of politics in order to – for lack of a better term – get rid of the bad weeds in government, whether they are bad politicians or bad policies.

And that's good. I commend you today for doing that.

133

We need that in our network of modern-day conservatives. We need the policy wonks, the numbers-crunchers, and the one-issue wonders to press the political powers-that-be continuously if we are going to improve our nation's capabilities as a global force.

However, with that said, whenever a nation finds itself in crisis, we must begin to not just look at the occasional weeds that need to be pulled up from the American harvest. We – as conservative leaders and as dedicated Americans – must begin to fully understand and act with patriotic love and honor on the premise that our American harvest – in many regards – is full of weeds. The soil of the American Way of Life has been diseased. For those that may disagree: just look around. The evidence is found in the crops all around us. Bad unemployment numbers. Bad schools. Youth apathy. Social tension. Hopelessness. Some of what is coming up through the American harvest today is truly rotten to the core and is unhealthy for consumption or growth.

When the harvest of America looks the way it does now – with the high unemployment, low workforce participation rates, lackluster academic performances, and lingering pessimism about American leaders and the direction they are taking us in – it's time for us to better understand the dynamics of this harvest. It's time for us to understand how the seeds of disappointment and discontent infiltrated the American homeland. It's time for us to act with more inclusive and insight chucks of knowledge so that we can denote where we went wrong as Americans – and even as conservatives....where we will learn from our mistakes and turn it around as a historic movement, and where we can humbly take America in the 21st century with our activism in the days ahead.

At one point of time or another in our lives – and notably since we got deeply involved in the American political discourse – we have heard someone....somewhere....throw around the term, "The American Way of Life", just as I did a bit earlier.

And, when we hear it, it sounds great, especially in a presidential election year or an Olympic year.

But, as we look at our current crop – a harvest full of strong weeds that are choking off the fruit of labor from generations on end - we have to ask: how many of us....or our neighbors....or our family members...or our friends...really understand what the "American Way of Life" truly means, particularly now in 2012?

Not many. Not anymore.

And that, sadly, is why so many of us – and particularly, so many of us that are the policy wonks, the numbers-crunchers, and the one-issue wonders that understand the complexities of policy purgatory and legislative angst...

That's why those noble and educated efforts often fall upon deaf ears, becoming nothing more than proverbial logs on the fire of partisan shouting matches that play well on television yet play out the string on an era of exceptionalism for the greatest nation this world has ever seen.

In order to be more effective in purporting the singular issues we support as conservative, free-market thinkers, we have to fully grasp the rudimentary issue that inhibits us from influencing others to open their minds to learning from us through engagement and debate.

The rudimentary issue facing us – the one that we must always remember as we discuss our principles and articulate their applications to real-life situations across this vast and diverse nation - is simply this: that although our battles are waged within the political arenas of our communities, the fight we must ensue and win is a cultural phenomenon.

Politics did not change our nation's perspective on the American Way of Life – the culture of America did over recent years. And when the culture of America altered what the American Way of Life constituted, it stripped us of critical elements within our make-up that are necessary to foster growth, health, and prosperity throughout our diverse nation.

Without a firm focus on the rudimentary issue and a persistent desire to heal the singed cultural foundation we face, no amount of impressive facts and figures that we have as free-market, conservative activists will make a difference in yielding more fruit in our increasingly-barren nation.

So what are we missing? What elements have been eroded away over time that, as a result, leave us in this condition as a people?

People may give a plethora of answers or suggestions, but most of them can be conceptualized and condensed down to what I have made the theme of these remarks. Unfortunately, in our beloved country today, we are fearful of...and, in some instances, fearful during...competition as Americans...

...we are failing with...and failing to optimize...our model of capitalism as Americans...

...and we are falling short in our outreach and articulation of our sense of free-market principles and conservative applications within America today.

Now, these shortcomings do not mean that we must give up on these things, as I will touch upon briefly. For example, our failures to optimize the power of our American capitalism do not mean that we hereby agree with our progressive fellow Americans. We don't believe that we must throw out capitalism. This is Americans for Prosperity. Americans for Socialism is the meeting down the hall to the left...the far left. There are some within our team of conservatives that present our ideas both effectively and passionately. We need more of those efforts, but to get there, we must also know what we are dealing with today.

If we commit to a methodical manner to engage the rudimentary cultural issue we face and maintain the tenacious pursuit of our beliefs and positions, we will find enough grace to heal America and plant the seeds for a robust renewal of our nation for our sunset years and our children's heyday for decades on end.

Simply put: we are dealing with an American society that needs us as conservative, free market thinkers and doers – from the policy wonks, the numbers-crunchers, and the one-issue wonders to the social media darlings and grassroots dynamos. We are dealing with an American society that needs us to show consistently – at the smallest level of debate to the grandest statements for our nation moving ahead – why they need us as free-market thinkers, as free-market leaders, and as free-market implementers to infuse good seed back into the American soil to rise up a more prosperous harvest.

The American Way of Life – as understood by many Americans today – does not include the desire to compete with vigor amongst each other as citizens and against the world as honest, hard-working brokers in the economic, education, and military endeavors we touch. Without a change in the cultural mindset, our cultural identity as the greatest nation in history will continue to erode into mediocrity.

Without the re-explanation and increased advocacy of the free-market principles that we extol in various areas, the cream of this nation can never truly rise to the top. With the languishing testing numbers and depressing drop-out totals that come from the school systems of Missouri and throughout the nation each year, only free-market principles being applied to struggling and apathetic school systems that have been short-changing both the treasure of our youth and the treasure of our tax dollars can change the dynamic of academic failure. With the woeful economic numbers in counties across the Mid-west despite federal and state-provided stimulus dollars for years now, only free-market principles pushing innovation, business leadership, civic climates, and community enhancements can foster hiring and the actual change we can believe in, instead of some catchy slogan that was cool 4 years ago but certainly is not now in this frosty employment environment.

Free-market principles understand optimizing capital, including human capital. Free-market principles understand that a just competition of an individual against one's self strengthens that individual and makes him better. Those principles purport that a just competition between two or more individuals strengthen both the parties involved and their communities as well.

But when a culture permeates fear to compete – when future scientists are no longer pushed in urban middle schools to outpace their previous academic performances and when businesses are no longer enabled to become leaner and meaner as corporate citizens and job providers – the seeds of free-market principles have no soil to take root. To win arguments as free-market thinkers in the general assemblies and in the halls of Congress – and even within the coffee shops of Jefferson City or Eureka – we must take on policy issues with a focus on the rudimentary cause of our situation today.

Our belief in the benefits of competition through applying free-market principles in education and economics will bolster the languishing understanding for the need of re-inspired capitalism in today's America as well. That system – an engine that has created the greatest amount of socioeconomic advancement in history – has been faltering without our active leadership to articulate its merits to all zip codes and neighborhoods. And it will continue to falter as long as we allow the rudimentary issue – a climate in America that inhibits competition and demonizes capitalism to the masses – to create the rules through which we impact our world politically.

We know free market principles create wealth and economic sustainability for Americans of all backgrounds when correctly understood and applied. Now, we must also address the cultural mood of this nation with our zeal for just competition. We must now apply it to the marketplace of the American mindset to robustly implement our beliefs for the sake of improving our nation. We must take advantage of this historically detrimental economy to bring our principles to new audiences and overcome all obstacles separating us from various voting blocs and challenge areas.

If we take on this challenge, we can win more elections and – more importantly – we can win back more impoverished areas and failing schools...we can win back neighborhoods plighted with violence and reclaim more Americans back into the fold as contributing citizens.

Those opportunities are there. Policy wonks, numbers-crunchers, and one-issue wonders: there are plenty of new audiences now waiting for your patriotic advocacy to change their lives for the better – even in the most unsuspecting of places.

As some of you may know, I was based in Chicago over the past 2 years due to my radio show, "Launching Chicago with Lenny McAllister." What you may not have known is that examples of our free market principles in action sometimes come about in the bastions of liberalism.

For example, Black leaders on the south side of the Windy City – from apolitical people such as the Minister Louis Farrakhan to old school, hard-core Democrats such as the Rev. Jesse Jackson, Sr and veteran Black nationalists – are promoting initiatives that encourage Chicago South-Siders to circulate their consumer resources around more times before the money leaves their neighborhoods. They are promoting initiatives that, by keeping this money in their communities a little longer, strengthen their purchasing power, force businesses to compete harder for market share and corporate partnerships, and make the communities more viable as equal partners in Chicago's overall economy.

Empowerment through economic competition and thoughtfulness. Revitalization through economic Darwinism within a marketplace. Prosperity expansion through creating wealth. This may be part of the Black agenda within Chicago but it fits into the scope of the free market principles that we purport for the advancement of the American people, not just Black people.
This example is one of many that show that, simply, our principles are above race and religion. They are American. They are timeless. And, when applied – they work.

Yet, in a culture that fears competition and fails to optimize our capitalistic message and meaning, our fight is more than just with policy positions. In the American society of today where bad-mouthing of our values – values that have empowered the poor around the world like never before in history – cannot be overcome because our focus is too much on articulating bullet points within our conservative movement, not foundational flaws that are uprooting the American Way of Life, we must change our perspective on what is truly going on in America.

141

Because some have allowed a fear to compete as Americans in schools and in business...in public discourse and in public service...to impede our advancement as a nation...we are forced to fight a cultural war through each individual political battle we take on.

Because we are falling short as free-market advocates to thoroughly pinpoint and explain the benefits of our vision and knowledge of capitalism and how it helps bankers and brick-layers alike...we are forced to fight a cultural war through each individual political battle we take on today.

That understanding is what I want us to take from these remarks and from this weekend: an understanding that in order to win the policy debates in today's America, we must foster a renewed passion to compete as Americans in order to discover the best around us and the best within us. As free market thinkers, we must present the merits of competition of choice in our schools, competition of products in our economic marketplaces, and the competition of ideas in the annuls of government at all levels. Without reclaiming the cultural war on the merits, we can never win the worthy battles that the policy wonks, the numbers-crunchers, and the one-issue wonders specialize in on our behalf.

Our understanding must be that for our successful system of capitalism to flourish to new heights in modern-day America, we must articulate and demystify our free market constructs to new audiences and constituencies, especially once we find out that they are aspiring to be like us without embracing the potential held in partnerships with us. Usually, without the conservative touch, the best intentions of liberals become government's most expensive-laid plans. With our perspective appropriately and proficiently implemented, the political specialists at the grassroots and professional levels become fully empowered to keep us on the proper course.

We are still capable of bringing about the changes this country needs. It is not too late to harvest a bountiful crop of innovation, economic revitalization, socioeconomic advancement, and appropriate government-citizen relations. However, we must be patriotic enough – and honest enough – to know that we – as free market thinkers and doers – are the ones that will heal the diseased soil of American culture so that good seed can once again take root from St. Louis to St. Clair County.

We must re-teach the American people to embrace competition as it is the pathway to the best of ourselves and our hidden potential.

We must re-apply American capitalism to a wider portion of Americans, so that our values can uplift both the lesser and more fortunate alike so this great but wounded nation can become greater still in the months and years ahead.

We must re-focus our efforts to take back America with both a grasp on policy positions and a renewed and improved grasp of the bigger picture: that the re-introduction of and recruitment for our values are on the forefront of this current American Revolution. Therefore, we must compete in all arenas with our values in tow. We must extol to all audiences free market solutions that make sense across our diverse nation. We must act with a zeal that knows that we are fighting political battles, but we are in the process of winning the cultural war – all done through the efforts of everyday Americans like you and me.

Thank you for this opportunity to speak with you today. God Bless your efforts as activists, the wonderful state of Missouri,
and God Bless the United States of America.

Hello, Tea Party Patriots! Good morning, my fellow Illinoisans! God Bless you, my fellow Americans!

Thank you for having me here today. I am glad that we can come together, once again, to share with each other the meaning of what makes the greatness of America so real for each one of us. It comes from the kindred spirit that we share. It comes from the common vision that we hold dear. It comes from the common resilience that freedom yields.

Now, before I go on, I want to say a few quick words. Say a few quick thank yous and set a brief ground rule or two.

First, thank you for your invitation to have me here today. Thank you to WMBD for having me on their airwaves both Monday afternoon as well as later today.

I want to thank my business partner, Chris Arps. He made the trip up from St. Louis to be here with us today. Thank you Chris.

Thank you to my ace, my wife Lannie, for her constant encouragement and love. She's back home in Chicago right now with our 2-year-old.

And further, let me say a very special thank you to Sheila Devall. By reaching out to me and working to make today possible, she proved once again that with modern technology, old-fashioned hope, and a little bit of God's grace, things happen. I'm glad to be here, and I thank you all for having me.

Now, I really don't have a lot of ground rules, but I do have two.

The first is that you don't hold against me the fact that I have written out my remarks. Let me briefly explain why I have prepared my remarks today.

I know that many of you have heard jokes about the presidential teleprompter. I don't want you to think that because I prepared my remarks, that maybe I just took a page out of the Chicago, big-eared, Black politician's Playbook. No, I did not. And generally, I don't do jokes about the teleprompter, so I won't now. Instead, I address why I have my methods...why it's important for me to prepare my remarks. I do it to confront a notion that is assigned to us conservatives by others.

Too often in America, conservatives are accused of having energy but no eloquence. We are told that we are passionate, yet we have no principles. We are accused of lacking substance and told that we have no statesmanship. We are characterized as a flash in the pan and not built to last. I am here today to say loudly and clearly: those claims are wrong.

Conservatives are energetic because of our love for the very best of America's values. That love is eloquent, passionate, and substantive. Conservatives are passionate because our concern for the future of America is founded in the disappointments of modern-day politics. Our passion is grounded in the ideals of this great nation, and it is genuine in wanting the best for our children and grandchildren. And our values – these conservatives values

146

we hold dear? They've built America and they are surely built to last.

And when they say we lack substance or statesmanship? Let me be clear: I feel that I have an obligation to you, to my family, to my community, and to our future…to prepare some remarks to refute and reject that falsehood about us. I want to show that…that something special about modern American conservatives. I want to highlight that the Tea Party movement, as we are called…has the statesmanship, the stewardship, and the leadership necessary to return the United States of America to its rightful place of international glory starting in 2012.

That's why I write out my remarks from time to time, so please understand.

Now, that gets me to my other ground rule.

We do not use today – or any other Tax Day moving forward – as a day to complain about the woes of our nation.

There are those throughout the land that will tell you and tell others: Tea Party conservatives are nothing more than complainers that don't want to pay their fair share…or don't like having a Black president…or don't want to do what is best for the United States of America.

To refute that, we must follow my other ground rule, starting today: do not be a complainer. Do not allow others to call you a complainer.

The Tea Party Movement is not about complaining about paying taxes or having a Black president or doing what some feel is best for the country, nor should this movement ever be concocted, directed, or hijacked in those directions. If we ever allow this sound movement to go off the rails completely and go in that direction, whether it be in your hearts and minds or in the media, we have lost the last, great opportunity to rescind the empty promises and bloated checks that American politics has given us over the past several decades.

We simply want fiscal responsibility in government with our tax dollars, not unmitigated and ongoing spending disasters in the halls of government. That is not complaining about taxes. That is speaking up for future generations of Americans before they are able to speak for themselves.

We simply want leadership that listens to and works with the people, not leadership that yields to crony politics when it comes to wasteful funding of Solyndra and the passing of the unconstitutional Obamacare healthcare reform bill. That is not racism. That is reminding the president, the House of Representatives, and the Senate that they work for the American people and must listen to the American people, not the other way around.

We simply want Springfield and Washington…Democrats and Republicans…neighbors and strangers…to have the insight to understand and the courage to enact the patriotic choices we face today. Doing what feels good for America is not always what *is* good for America. Spending more on bureaucracy at the local, state, and national levels has yielded diminishing returns for our communities, our schools, our business climate, and our way of doing politics in our nation. Doing what is best for our nation is not always doing what is popular in our nation.

Therefore, we will endure the name-calling. We will endure the taunts. We will persevere past the tension in these times. But, we will do so by following the second ground rule….and rejecting that we are complainers.

Let me assure you: we are not complainers. We are patriotic. We are courageous. And we will win this battle for America's soul and for the nation's prosperous future.

America is not a nation of complainers. Complainers do little more than…well…complain.

They are the Monday morning quarterbacks. They are the couch potatoes of the world. They are the ones seeing their bellies grow and can feel the shortness of breath coming on from being out of shape, but they just refuse to put down the potato chips and cheese dip to get active and get involved.

Complainers are inactive. Americans – and particularly the Tea Party Movement…folks such as you all here today – are active, engaged, and inspiring.

Americans – and particularly the Americans standing with us today – are protestors, proactively looking to make a difference in the communities around them with a patriotism that we should have a long time ago...but we are certainly glad that it's not too late to have here in 2012.

Therefore, my two ground rules:

Please understand why I have prepared remarks for today. I feel that we have an obligation to show downstate Illinois and others through the nation that we are stately in our patriotism and poised in our march to take back America.

As well, please avoid idle complaining on Tax Day and allowing others to call you a complainer. You are a patriotic protestor, using class, decorum, and the Constitution to protest dysfunction in government and win back the future for our children and grandchildren.

After all, if we are going to win back the future, we have to start winning today. Thus, 2012 is not a year for continuing old trends. 2012 is not the end of a 4-year journey to vote out a president and, in essence, return Washington to Americans and return a Chicagoan to Chicago.

Although I hear that this move could certainly help some things.

If we are going to win back the future, 2012 cannot be a continuation of the same old, same old or the endpoint of a narrow-minded strategy or goal.

Instead, I tell you: 2012 must stand for a new beginning, a new hope, and better change.

When I thought about titling these remarks, this theme – A New Beginning, A New Hope, and Better Change – came to me. I know that I am constantly in the process of securing better change for my family and my loved ones. I find myself at the beginning of new personal and spiritual cycles for further extending my faith in God, myself, and this country.

To have better change…to have new hope…I had to realize that where I am right now…and, I propose, where we are as a nation right now…must be the platform we use to project ourselves forward into winning the future. Regardless of how broken we are as a nation – or how broke we are as individuals due to this ongoing recession – we must use where we are right now as the new beginning…with an understanding and a new perspective on what 2012 truly is.

2012 is not an election year for resetting American politics; it's an intention year for setting the roadmap for the future of America. It is more than just about who we vote for in November. It is about whom we have become recently and who we want to be moving forward. This is not just about voting out one set of politicians for another. This is all about ushering in a new, more efficient, more responsive, and more effective set of politics, starting in 2012.

With a new beginning starting today with proactive protesting, not complaining…

…with a new hope that you are the difference that America needs for a lifetime, not for just one moment in time…

…with a new perspective and understanding that you are the leaders of America, not merely led like sheep to the slaughterhouse of national dysfunction…

…together, we can usher in conservative principles, appropriate government, and a better change for America and our future, instead of the change we shouldn't believe in that we were sold 4 long years ago.

Therefore, when I say "new hope and better change", don't go back to the days of 2008 and the hope and change from the liberals. Instead, think of a safer bastion of liberalism, for just one moment – one that we all occasionally enjoy:

Hollywood.

Go back into your childhoods. Remember the story of a group of rag-tag misfits, scattered across time and space, taking on the fight for freedom against an establishment empire, a formidable foe with countless resources, and years of domination on their side.
And even manipulation of an invisible force?

Yes, I am talking about Star Wars, circa 1977, Episode 4:

A New Hope.

And no, although some Tea Party patriots like going around dressed like the founding fathers, I'm not asking you to pull out your R2D2 or Princess Leia costumes anytime soon. What I am saying, though, is that even in the smallest and most entertaining of things, life imitates art which inspires life.

An establishment empire with years of domination on their side? Doesn't that sound like the liberal, big government, big spending, big bureaucracy American systems of politics, education, and taxation that are dominating our country today? And, if you think about Darth Vader's death grip, it does seem as though these things are, just as well, choking the life out of what made America great years ago.

And what about that rag-tag group of folks spread across a region that seemingly didn't fit together? Those heroes had many differences and disagreements but, in the end, they made it work through a common goal and a common sense of destiny and freedom. Doesn't that sound like the people gathered here today…shouldn't that be what this Tea Party movement should be all about? Enough differences to keep us interested. Enough commonality to keep us focused. Enough love for our destiny of freedom to make us successful.

2012 may not be our Star Wars or Hollywood moment, per se, for we don't do this for the cameras. However, it certainly must be a new beginning for a new hope...if we are to win back the future and take back America.

2012 must be a new beginning with new hope, but that hope cannot be limiting or narrow-minded. It is very easy to think that 2012 is merely about November. If November is your endpoint, today is not your beginning. If January 2013 is your endpoint, 2012 is not your beginning.

Those of us that understand that 2012 is our beginning also know that America's future – and better change for that future – is our endpoint. And the graceful thing that God gives us with this understanding is that this endpoint is a never-ending evolution into the best that we can be. It allows us to be protestors in the proactive sense of our American history, not be complainers and couch potatoes. It emboldens us to be historic in our patriotism, not to be haughty in our activism. It shows us that bringing about a better change for America can have different methods and techniques, even with the same time-tested values that have made the diverse American people the envy of the world.

My fellow Americans, this year...2012...cannot just be a rallying cry for a new president or a shift in Washington or Springfield. 2012 must be a launching point...a new beginning for a better change that elevates the future through honoring and embracing the best aspects of our conservative past.

We bring better change through being proactive, through protesting, and through patriotism by way of events such as today. It's in our national DNA. It's what we do. It's how we inspire. It's how we succeed as a people.

In the 1700s, the colonists did not merely complain about the contentions between the King of England and the settlers in the original 13. They protested. They enacted what they believed. They sacrificed – and against an establishment empire with countless resources – they won.

In the 1800s, the defenders of freedom and conscientiousness did not merely complain about the evils of slavery and its toxic impact on America's young fiber. They protested. They were active. They put their lives on the line though the abolition movement and through fighting to protect the promise of a new, fragile, but potentially great nation. They sacrificed – and against an established lifestyle and with America's future on the line – they won and re-united the USA.

In the 1900s, Americans did not merely complain about the evils of Nazi Germany or the perils of the Jim Crow South or the dangers of the communist Soviet Union. They protested in an active way. They marched. They fought. They liberated and they inspired. They sacrificed – and against the rhetoric that they were facing long odds or decades of status quo or the threat of nuclear annihilation – they won and the world benefited because of it.

And because they won, we won. And because they protested then, we protest now. And because they stood up then, we have no recourse but to stand up now. And because they withstood tension in the past to give our generations a sturdy today, we will resist the animus now with honor and humble righteousness to use 2012 as the new beginning to give the next generations a better change for a stronger tomorrow.

A better change from this new beginning comes from more than just changing out political players in the game. It comes from changing the dynamic that politics IS a game. The better change comes from changing the mindset that tax revenue is Monopoly money to be wasted carelessly. The better change comes from changing the mindset that major decisions in government are made only after hand-selected big-wigs cast their political dice to see who gets your representatives' attention…over you. The better change comes from changing the mindset that political leadership is about doubling-down on sound bites and Beltway in-fighting instead of listening to the people they were supposed to represent.

American politics…American governments across the land…are not games for the privileged. They are gateways of freedom for the people of this land. With this new beginning in 2012, those in office will act as the defenders of the gateways that they are…or they will see just how much of game-changers the American people will be with the 2012 elections and beyond.

A better change from this new beginning understands that it is our obligation to the future…our duty to our ancestors…our task in taking back America…

…we are required to hold and succeed through the tough conversations to address the national debt, racial inequality, struggling economic recovery, much-needed educational improvements, social contention in communities, and political dysfunction in government.

We believe that 2012 is the new beginning. As conservatives, we inspire America to have a new hope for a better future. And we – this gathering here in Illinois as well as our kindred gathered throughout the nation today – understand that through our love of America, our decorum with fellow Americans today, and our vision for future Americans henceforth, we will soon bring about a better change to win the future. We will win through applying the very best of our conservative past and enabling the love and innovation of today's leaders – the American people.

I believe in the new beginning granted to us by God here in 2012. I believe in the new hope for a stronger America through our protest and our activism, through our inspiration from the past and our inspiring actions for the future. I believe that by being involved and by staying educated and engaged proactively, we will win elections, we will win more hearts and minds around this nation, but most importantly – we will win the future and take back America.

America is not a color. In the red, white, and blue of our flag can be found shades of tan, brown, black, and white.

America is not a nation of cowards or complainers. In the melting pot of this great country can be found the ingredients of revolution, the substance of liberty and prosperity, the bread of life from our God-based values, and the spice of life from our diversity.

And finally, let us be clear: America is not the land where conservatism came to die in this world. In you – in our new beginning of 2012, our new hope found in your efforts and activism, our better change for the future by the work of your hands…

…in you…is everything that we need to change the national conversation, improve the dysfunction in government, transform past disappointment in politics, and scale back the blood-letting of the public dole of our tax dollars.

In us is everything we need to liberate the innovation that makes America great. In us is everything we need to heal the generations of young people of all colors and all creeds that are looking for empowering hope and change that they can get from conservatives like us starting in 2012, not the nope and cringe that they have been getting over the past 4 years.

They need what we can offer with our new beginning in 2012, not the hopelessness and confusion that they have right now.

My fellow Americans, in 2012, you symbolize that new hope. In 2012, you light the pathway to that better change for us all. In 2012, you are that bridge to winning the future. Starting right now in 2012, I embrace that new beginning, and I ask you to join me in doing so.

I do so because I believe in you, and I believe that through our conservative efforts, America – across racial lines, religious creeds, socioeconomic classes, and educational backgrounds – will win the future – together. I trust our commitment to winning the future. I know that we have what it takes to win the future. And I believe in you and the greatness of these United States. So, let's go do it, starting with the new beginning granted today in 2012.

Thank you for this opportunity to speak with you today.
God Bless you. God Bless the state of Illinois,
And God Bless the United States of America.

Good morning, fellow patriots! God Bless you, my fellow Americans! How are you doing today?

Are you fired up to take back your government?

Are you prepared to take back the greatness of the American Dream?

Are you ready to be patriotic, historic, and victorious for the sake of future Americans?

That's good. In fact, it's more than good – it's fantastic.

Thank you for having me here today at The Patriot Field of Dreams.

Let me say a few quick thank yous before we start.

Thank you to Kim Paris and all the work she has done with organizing this event and working with me concerning being here with you today.

I want to say thanks to the leadership and members of Move-On-Up.

Thanks to grassroots advocates such as Linda Ragsdale and the folks at Americans for Prosperity.

I also want to thank the other wonderful patriots that hosted me and befriended me while I have been here in the Show Me State.

I speak to you here from what the Rally for Common Sense Committee has named "The Arena of Ideas Stage." This is the place where we the speakers talking to you today are asked to push We the People gathered here in Holts Summit…

…we are asked to push you and push ourselves intellectually, instructionally, and interactively from this stage. We are asked as speakers to not only rally the conservative troops for a difference at the ballot box in November. We are asked as leaders and as Americans to challenge ourselves – challenge all of us, in fact – to commit to a political change back to liberty, to sensible government, to statesmanship in politics, and to American Exceptionalism for 2012 and for years to come.

As we celebrate our common commitment to our future as a nation and our impending victories in government as conservatives, I share with you my personal celebration today.

It was exactly 10 years ago that I embraced the essence of the pursuit of happiness that was endeared by America's Founding Fathers and captured in the words of the Declaration of Independence - that literary spark that gave rise to the brightest and boldest nation to ever illuminate the skies of history.

See: against what bureaucrats said, against what the statistics predicted, against what my family background dictated, and against what my socioeconomic status afforded, conservative principles overcame progressivism and melancholy.

An unmarried African-American father, raising 2 young children…under his roof, post-divorce and post-9/11…fighting as his own attorney against the wiles of judicial activism…fighting against the social and bureaucratic struggles that usually asphyxiate Black children's hopes and aspirations with broken homes and broken dreams…

…that American walked his two children – ages 8 and 2 years old – across a college stage and picked up his college degree after nearly a decade and a half of academic toils, dropping out of school to care for sick parents, working as a deli clerk and as a janitor to support his young family…all while chasing the dream of a better life because of the opportunities provided through the American Dream.

That was possible – for my family and for my children and grandchildren – because conservative principles and the ability to pursue happiness and the American Dream are still possible here in our great nation due to the time-tested values that we hold dear.

As long as conservatives such as us gathered here today continue to protect the true essence of the American Dream and the foundation of that Dream – our bold federal Constitution – these stories will continue today and everyday around the country. And with these stories come the promise of the comeback of the American people. With these stories come the solutions we need for a stronger America, instead of more promises coming from 4 more years from a nope and cringe president or a budget-less, do-little Senate.

Today, we are asked to do more than just bolster our patriotism through the honor of gathering together at this noble rally.

We are asked to be intellectual with our debates as we convince our wayward countrymen that we love this nation and, therefore, we must change the course from this destructive path that we are on right now.

We are asked to be instructional with our rhetoric so that we not only fire up this crowd here today. We also build a fire that warms up younger generations today and future generations of Americans in the days ahead. To succeed, our fiery passion must warm up new generations of Americans to conservative values, conservative leadership, and patriotic service in the halls of government.

We are asked to be interactive with our words, with our actions, with our love for you as children of God and our love for each other as fellow Americans. We must do these things if the fire that we are building today is to become the zeal necessary to blaze a new path of greatness for the melting pot of America in the 21st century.

We know that our diverse, talented, and expansive nation cannot triumph past our financial woes if we count on big government to provide its version of leadership and vision for success. Big government cannot provide these things effectively.

Has big government fixed our struggling educational systems that impact our children throughout America? Has big government spending capped the heights of unemployment nationally at 8% as we were told in 2009?

We need small government and bigger people in America to elevate American Exceptionalism once again. We need a historical sense of the appropriate roles of government, family, education, economic liberty and multi-lateral prosperity in the United States today. We need to push away politicians that seek to be popular for all of the wrong reasons and promote Americans that choose to be historic by serving us for all of the right reasons.

Therefore, the purpose of my talk with you today is not just to fire you up with talking points or television-ready sound bites.

All of us speakers can remind you of just who you are. You all – are the WE THE PEOPLE that America is pleading for to return to leadership today.

All of us can remind you of who the people are that need you…that need you to be historic and be humble, servant leaders in whatever way you can starting today. You all – you are the last true hope for the huddled masses, yearning to breathe free –

away from the oppression of status quo civics and away from the hopelessness of unresponsive and bloated government.

All of us can articulate – whether it is with a preacher's passion or politician's eloquence – the power of your presence here today. You all – you are the humble points of light that illuminate this Patriot Field of Dreams with the resonance of your potential. You have awakened a sleeping people and invigorated an apathetic nation to remember…who we are, what we do, and why we must go forth from here.

We are the United States of America. We lead as the greatest source of economic, military, and altruistic good that the world has ever seen.

And we must go forth from here as conservatives to gain political ground, win political conversations, and win back apathetic hearts and minds so that we can win back our future and take back America.

That's why I would fail you while on this stage today - if I did not challenge you for the sake of America's future, not just remind you of our conservative values of the past.

This Rally for Common Sense is a rally on behalf of an uncommon people. And because this rally is on behalf of the most unique nation in the history of man, we cannot settle for merely convincing our fellow conservatives that our cause is just. We must also be commissioned to reclaim the areas that we have lost to progressive, overbearing, and expensive government and its tentacles of bureaucracy over the past several decades.

Patriots, we can rally to win a skirmish, but we must sacrifice in order to win back our future and take back America.

We are challenged with the question: what are we truly willing to sacrifice for liberty and American Exceptionalism to endure in its purest sense in the 21st century?

We are commissioned to act courageously as we answer the question: where must we go in order to truly impact change, truly reduce the size of government, sincerely revitalize American innovation, and proudly extol the American Dream?

We cannot take back America from the influence of government corruption and cronyism if we refuse to take on Chicago-style politics, whether it's found in the White House in Washington, the state house in Jefferson City, or the city halls found throughout the Land of Lincoln and the hometowns through the USA.

We cannot reduce spending on outdated models of education, job creation, community activism, and public service while increasing our harvests from all four of those fields…if we allow the outdated model in our own political camp to continue. We must reject the notion immediately that suggests that conservative principles only have certain zip codes or that the American Dream has borders in our land.

I tell you from this Arena of Ideas Stage – the stage is set for you, my fellow Americans and my conservative compatriots –

the stage is set for you to apply your intellect to American political discourse each day. The stage is set for you to inform and to illustrate to our people that the conservative way is still the best way to access the American Way of life.

It always has been, regardless of whether you were a poor Black grandchild of former slaves that ended up becoming a doctor…or if you were a European immigrant that went from manual labor to millionaire status within one generation.

I implore you on this gorgeous May day – the time is now for you to instruct others of the tenets of conservatism, the promise of our philosophy, the goodness of the founding principles of this nation, and the greatness that America can still claim in the 21st century if only we return to the best of our past to make a better future.

Rallying our conservative troops is no longer enough. It is time for us to love these United States enough to reclaim more Americans from the disjointed legacy of big, expensive, wasteful, and unresponsive government that dictates too many lives today and influences too many young voters for tomorrow.
I ask you as a brother in Christ and as a fellow American, understand and embrace the notion that we must be interactive with our patriotism, not just involved in the fight.

A nation like ours is worth fighting for, indeed. But it is even more than that. It is a society built through the interactive toils of "We the People" headlined in the US Constitution. It provides a freedom that comes when we instruct and remind both the oldest conservative and the neophyte liberal alike that this nation was founded and has endured because of the sake of liberty from government to pursue happiness in life. It elicits an honor that comes when our love for this nation is intellectualized, empowering us – and even commissioning us – to evangelize the promise of America to the apathetic and the broken around you, not just preach to the choir here today.

In order to succeed truly in 2012 and beyond, I ask you, I encourage you…and I challenge us all – to not only recite the good news of our values to the conservative church gathered in our circles, but to take the Gospel of American Exceptionalism to those that need it the most – and to those that need US the most. It is time to reclaim our American Dream, but to do so, we must take back America by taking our message to America. It is time to meet those that lost hope for America in the streets. It is time for our patriotism to expand into courageous activism. It is time for us to meet our future where it is and take it to where we need them to go – so that we can rise to where America belongs…as the shining city on a hill in this world once again.

It is time to embrace the moment here in this Patriots Field of Dreams, fellow Americans, but in holding this moment dear, grasp the potential of what this nation will be because of you in 2012 and beyond.

Embrace the reformation of better education for our kids through more efficient programs such as school vouchers.

Embrace the newfound innovation of American workers through tax codes that support entrepreneurs and opportunities that utilize the resurgence of American intellect.

Embrace the modern-day Reagan Recovery coming soon where, through your efforts, a diversity of jobs allow blue collar workers to buy houses with honor and allow college-educated workers to build legacy within the American Dream.

Embrace your obligation to reclaim the ground that we have lost over the past decades in our streets, in our neighborhoods, in our cities, and in our communities.

Embrace the new future. Embrace your destiny as the reason why America resurges as THE global force of the 21st century.

Embrace American Exceptionalism. Resurge the hope of the American Dream in our everyday lives.

Embrace conservatism and seize the day!

Thank you for this opportunity to speak with you today.
God Bless this Patriot Field of Dreams.
God Bless the state of Missouri,
And God Bless the United States of America.

Fighting for Choice While Eliminating Choices

DC Mayor Vincent Gray's arrest over the budget debate shows again the dysfunction over what Black America choose to fight over.

Sorry.

Some may see Washington DC Mayor Vincent Gray's recent arrest while protesting budget cuts for his city as heroic, noble, and necessary.

I don't. In fact, I view it as quite the opposite in many ways. Couple this with the recent arguments coming from much of Black America – including the recent protests here in Chicago over billboards and the fight by African-Americans to continue federal funding of Planned Parenthood while education funds are being cut (and often agreed to by both political parties) – and it all seems to epitomize the very essence of what's wrong with Black America today.

Too often, we stand up for the wrong things for the sake of political correctness and doing what we are expected to do without looking at the long-range impact for the communities due to our stances. Gray's recent protest a few weeks ago was against the current deal cut by politicians on Capitol Hill. This deal highlighted two big items: a cut to federal funding of abortions in Washington, DC and a return of the DC School Choice/Voucher program - both initiatives spearheaded by Republicans in the House of Representatives. Both items are vehemently opposed by Gray. Of course, upon looking at the issues, one would have to conclude that this has nothing to do with people but has everything to do with politics.

Standing up for government-funded abortions and protesting against school vouchers in educationally-failing Washington, DC has less to do with values within the collective Black community than it does with the political allegiances of the collective Black community. In following lock, stock, and barrel with the whims of two of the biggest lobbying factions of the Democrat "progressive" base – the pro-"choice" lobbying base (a base that, ironically, only seems to push the choice of abortion to our communities) and the teachers' unions- too many of us are willing to forfeit our future in order to win today's political battles.

And, in essence, we are willing to be both pro-choice and anti-choice all at the same time, a contradiction that rapidly leads us down the road of irrelevancy and, quite possibly, practical civic extinction.

It's not a coincidence that the biggest fight on Capitol Hill – the one that almost shut down the government to the chagrin of the nation and to the heightened dismay to the Black community that disproportionately relies on the federal government for basic living from employment to benefits – centered on the pro-Planned Parenthood funding debate. Of course, to get most of us on-board with this fight, the context was wrapped in the guise of being another civil rights issue that Black Americans should run to the rescue to, all while ignoring one of the primary civil rights issues from America's past – educational equality.

Lock, stock, and barrel – we collectively fell for it again.

At some point, when do we ignore the partisan altar calls coming from Washington, even when they are conveniently labeled "basic rights" issues that basically do not change the conditions found in most Black working class communities today?

Funding of Planned Parenthood or abortions in Washington, DC are not paramount issues that will overturn the culture of crisis and death within Black America that is strangling our youth.

Educational inequalities and ineffectiveness do. Unless more Black Americans are willing to exert the same amount of vigor and veracity of concern with items of education as they are with the liberal voting agenda, we will continue to follow down the path of the partisan pied pipers that come along, all while leaving the American political and social landscape in the near future without much more than a song and a dance and nothing else for our future – if we are even so lucky to have one.

We Are the Change

Yes: the way some political folks act makes you wanna <u>scream</u>*,*
but more often than not, the only way to make a change is to stick
around long enough <u>to fight the powers that be.</u>

If memory serves me correctly, I had an opportunity to meet <u>Dee</u>
<u>Dee Blasé</u> not too long ago. I do believe one such occasion was in
Arizona during the 2010 <u>SB 1070 controversy</u> that captured the
nation's attention.

I have followed Dee Dee's dedication to the causes of Latinos in
America and admired her authenticity concerning these efforts. I
have followed her <u>organizational efforts</u> as well as the <u>troubles</u> that
her journey has encountered.

From what I know, Dee Dee is a well-intended American. I
commend her commitment to her beliefs. I wish her well in her
endeavors in trying to make America a better and stronger nation.

And I ask her to return to the Republican Party.

I understand that to many readers, this sounds like nothing more
than a party hack asking another brown face to join (or, in this
case, rejoin) the GOP in order to beat back the <u>image of</u>
<u>intolerance</u> that stung the party during the 2008 RNC Convention
in Minnesota. That's hardly the case. I can clearly relate to the
oft-accumulating mounds of frustration that comes with being a
minority within a political party that has the right policy
perspectives but also has <u>pockets of insensitive</u> (or, in some case,
oblivious) leadership in regards to race. Yet, I also know that
whenever change is needed, it is not prompted from outside of
the system; it is primed – and even demanded – from within.

I have said it to others before the Justin Velez-Hagan <u>piece hit the</u>
<u>internet days ago</u>, and I repeat it now: minority Republicans need

to stop running from the political fight if they ever truly want to win the social fights that hamper our nation.

And yes, if you really thought about it, you would realize that you need to be making that case to them as well, regardless of how racist or intolerant you think the GOP is.

It disheartens me from time to time whenever I hear of good Republicans leaving the GOP because of the stonewall of intolerance that is found at varying levels of regional and state parties. The levels of frustration are understandable, but the call to make history and the obligation to the past are both greater in resonance than the power that any angry moment could ever muster. Simply put, with each minority Republican that leaves the party out of a sense that the party will never change, the worst fears of maintaining status quo within the political circles – and subsequently, the social arenas in which we live – are closer to being crystallized into the American fabric for generations to come.

Sadly, most minority voting blocs have always fought the American heavyweight championship battle known as politics with one arm tied behind their backs, whether it was during Reconstruction (because of Jim Crow racism) or after the Great Society Movement that solidified our collective voting state today. How is the underclass expected to effectively wrestle an opponent with the ever-changing speed of Muhammad Ali in his youth and the awesome power of Mike Tyson in his youth, doing so with the limiting handicap of one-sidedness? It can't. It won't. It loses now – and, on this path, it loses for the foreseeable future.

Political balance becoming a reality anytime soon will not occur if the soldiers best equipped to fight for political equality for our communities fail to stick around to win the battle. Say what you want about the freedom of being labeled an independent or the power of non-partisan groups in today's America. In a government that has been built for centuries with money, tradition, and geopolitical reinforcement with the intent to support and substantiate a two-party system of legislative power in America, the paramount method to solidify and grow meaningful and long-lasting influence is to incorporate oneself into the system and be steadfast in one's beliefs and goals in the process. Being involved and not being a sellout is the key. Any alternative is nothing more than taking a bullhorn to shout at the building with the rallying thousands in the streets when nothing less than a seat at the table will prompt the necessary conversations and subsequent political and social changes that we seek and require to succeed in 21st Century America. There may be a lot of gnashing of teeth going through this, but gnashing of teeth to endure the frustration puts change in a position to never bite one's tongue in the presence of history during the most critical moments to initiate positive and empowering change.

It might have been said on the other side of the aisle, but it is a true statement: we are the change that we seek. And because we are that change, we cannot and must not run from our obligation to get our hands dirty and our feet worn, just as our forefathers just several generations ago did not retreat from getting their hands bloodied or their bodies battered for the sake of reclaiming justice in our world. So, I will be here, ready and willing to fight for upliftment of all people and notably for the underclass through whatever political and societal means necessary. Because I know other minority Republicans love people as well, I expect the Dee Dee Blases and others within the minority conservative realm to return beside me so that, by going "all in" with our communities on some key issues, we can uplift America to a better place as soon as possible.

A Pound of Hubris when an Ounce of Humility Would Do

A cautionary tale for Black conservatives: even if the allegations are not true (a big "if" to some at this point), Herman Cain's demeanor and responses to them are not winning over many Americans to his views or his leadership.

Where is Ricky Ricardo when you need him? Somebody needs to let GOP presidential candidate Herman Cain know that he has some 'splainin' to do.

No, it's not just in regards to the sexual allegations that Mr. Cain adamantly denied over the course of the week by way of a press conference in Arizona. Yes, that is plenty enough explaining that he will need to do, covering not just allegations that stretch from Chicago to Washington, DC, but as well for the hopes for supporters that are rooting for this candidacy to survive this significant storm.

There's some "splanin'" that must come forth regarding other Cain issues yielding a not-too-complimentary image of the Cain Train, even if his momentum of support has maintained in many ways thus far.

For example, explain this: for a man that has often noted that he is the only non-politician running for the presidency on the Republican ticket, the amount of political hubris that Mr. Cain has shown over the course of the past 2 weeks has reflected less of the grassroots affability (and perhaps even some sense of humility) that allowed him to string together straw poll wins starting in Florida 2 months ago. Instead, it comes off with the same image of the proud, us-versus-them mentality that creates more enemies than friends and creates more apathy towards American politics. The stonewalling efforts fending off the allegations of harassment have been criticized for the damaging double-talk from Cain while the story grew, from differing stories

176

on settlements to recollections about the details surrounding these allegations. However, more damaging (and often less discussed) to Cain's image is the arrogant manner in which he has denied the claims. During the infamous November 8 press conference from Arizona, Cain denied ever meeting one of the accusers just weeks after seeing the woman in a back-stage encounter in Chicago, then turned around and called the woman a "troubled woman" sent by Democrats to destroy his campaign in a plea similar to one made by a master politician a decade ago. Of course, in a manner perhaps saved only for presidential politicians, Cain's defiance against this conspiracy came after standing up to the "other perpetrator" that leaked this story to the media in a political hit against the campaign.

Explanations fending off a firestorm have never been spoken more accusatorily by a career politician.

Yet, more damage to the folksy feel-good nature of the Cain Train was caused later in the week with his unnecessary ribbing of former Speaker of the House "Princess" Nancy Pelosi during the GOP debate in Michigan. This comment came at a time when he should have been more mindful of his slip in the polls (particularly with women) that dropped him into a virtual tie with GOP presidential competitors Mitt Romney and Newt Gingrich. At the very least, it should have become mindful enough to avoid any further comments or actions that could be construed as condescendingly sexist, arrogant, or unpresidential.

Of course, if the only tarnish of hubris on the Cain finish recently came while addressing the set of allegations, it would be enough. However, this manner pilots a dangerous pattern that threatens not only his campaign, but risks squandering another opportunity for Black conservatives to make headway in America.

Instead of attacking the left consistently with facts and figures as he so eloquently did when addressing President Clinton and the universal health care movement in the 1990s, Cain increasingly chooses to resort to name-calling and insults that lead to both a round of applause with conservative circles and diminishing returns regarding respect and dignity among the American electorate he would have to serve as president. This mindset also led to Cain repeatedly taking on the Occupy Wall Street protestors and the issues they raise (perhaps incorrectly at times) by stating arrogantly that they only have themselves to blame if they are struggling in America during these economic woes, all while Mr. Cain quickly reminds Republican primary voters that these complaints are rooted in self-accountability deficiencies and Obama-led policies.

The self-accountability position plays well for Cain, a stance that is acceptable generally but is often dangerously misapplied concerning race as Mr. Cain continues capturing GOP primary voters' and America's collective attention. Cain's denouncement of the existence of racism in modern America - complete with comments about how White conservatives can't fake liking him for this length of time and how his "flavor of the week" status made him "Black Walnut" - trivializes modern racial disparities and reflects the stances concerning post-racism held by many Black conservatives. Of course, this becomes colored with duplicity when many of the same people defend Cain against "high-tech lynchings", emphatic efforts made by pundits and those espousing the plights of Black conservatives to the point of being both haughty and laughable. Anytime the Rev. Al Sharpton is able to criticize accurately the arrogant hypocrisy of racism claims by Cain and his supporters concerning the current campaign crisis, it should be clear that the train is rapidly being driven from the tracks.

And it is not just the Cain Train that is threatening to derail. There is a clear explanation for both the recent Cain campaign faux pas and, perhaps, there is a bigger lesson here for Black conservatives in general. Basically, ***know your place.***

I emphatically state that I am <u>not</u> referring to the backroom, <u>mascot-level status</u> that many Black Americans believe Black Republicans and conservatives serve in today's political climate. What I am referring to, however, is the dais of responsibility that Black conservatives must claim in this era to confront the political and social competition before them to win with facts, valor, and statesmanship.

What Cain has forgot on his way to the top of the polls is often what many Black conservatives forget when dealing within the political arena today: regardless of the <u>detestable</u> and <u>inflammatory behavior</u> that their political foes may engage in, Black conservatives are not in a position to reciprocate the status quo in any way due to the current crisis within America, not to mention the current status of Black conservatives within America today. At a time when leadership, poise, and balance are sorely needed within America in general and Black America particularly, Black conservatives are not afforded the leeway to come across as either <u>stereotypical in their "patriotism"</u> or <u>arrogant and detached in their political delivery</u>. Black conservatives cannot claim Martin Luther <u>King, Jr. as a Republican</u> and ignore King's sentiment on <u>love driving out hate</u> through a de facto strategy of taking on political adversaries with hateful and hurtful insinuations of <u>brainwashing</u> and <u>work ethic</u> concerning Black and liberal America. When it happens, Black conservatives risk further becoming a tool of the right and the scorn of the left, both without having much power to impact necessary change in Black America or anyplace else within our nation in need. More Americans are in critical need today and, thus, more is required of the Black conservative than just regurgitating the status quo that we already get from political operatives and politicians.

Leadership is not pointing out the symptoms of the social epidemic without providing both the solutions *and* required patience needed for partnerships to deliver people to a better place. Just the same, humble, servant leadership from Black conservatives at a time when Black support of President Obama has been waning for months cannot be curtailed by finger-waving, emotionally-charged rounds of bravado enacted in the process of making one's point. Ironically, the same critique that many Black conservatives make concerning Black Democrats now epitomizes the very vices choking the moral momentum away from Black conservatism in general. From a more immediate perspective, it takes away from the Cain Train momentum to the nomination in Tampa.

To get back on track, Mr. Cain, remember that leadership can be described as a gift that comes like a liquid. Open and steady hands provide stability to capture and maintain leadership within one's grasp. The pounding of fists through arrogance or heavy-handedness allows leadership to slip through one's fingers. Grasp this before it is too late. For Black conservatives in general, perhaps it is a lesson that we should heed as well before it is too late for us to fully grasp this opportunity for proper and needed change.

Challenging the NAACP, Condemning the Tea Party Express, yet Confronting the Truth on Contemporary Racism

President Ben Jealous and the NAACP sound like they're backing off, and the Tea Party Express got the boot from the Tea Party Federation, but without some real talk on where we are as a nation, we merely balk from opportunities to improve ourselves

I have been watching all of the colorful (pun intended) sights and sounds from the past week, wondering when did I walk into the 1960s all of the sudden – or, worse still, some altered version of the 1960s where civil rights organizations get it wrong on race, wholesome Americans get represented by a world-class bigot, and Black people turn a blind eye to the deteriorating racial conditions within America by proclaiming that "institutionalized racism is dead."

Between the Tea Party resolution last week and the embarrassment surrounding the Shirley Sherrod controversy this week, it is clear that the NAACP is scrambling to get its footing on how to address issues impacting race relations in America in the 21st century. Although they are struggling to find the best path for communicating and addressing these issues as they try to dodge being "snookered" again into a race controversy, it is evident that leadership within the proud organization has allowed itself to be "bamboozled" into taking on racial confrontations without the necessary set of facts to be effective. Because of that, the NAACP should have been challenged, not only by conservative bloggers and activists that are looking for fair standards and definitions of racial protocol in today's America, but also by urban Americans and people of color that have leaned on the NAACP as a pillar of moral authority for decades. Pushing the organization to transcend the times with creative methods for engagement and resolution of problems should be encouraged, even as the NAACP was persuaded to take the bait to stand in opposition to the Tea Party and its oft-reported and under-actualized racism.

Of course, Mark Williams and the Tea Party Express made the grassroots conservative movement an easy target, as Williams' multiple comments were peppered with toxic sentiments that highlighted an overt anger towards African-Americans. His comments comparing the NAACP's non-profit status and its $20 million budget unfavorably to slave traders' profit margins were repugnant, especially considering the mission of each set of endeavors. Williams' "satirical" letter written as "Ben Jealous" showed that ignorance may be bliss, but awareness of one's poisonous influence displays a treachery that must not be ignored. Having Tea Party Express expelled from the Tea Party Federation is a good step, but without these patriots opening their collective mind to what is transpiring in America, the doors of opportunity for healing this nation past the impending explosion of massive episodes of 21st century racial, economic, and social discord throughout the country will continue to close rapidly.

Proclamations that "institutionalized racism is dead" and other forms of defiance against both the NAACP and the Tea Party Express do not confront the truth that is before us in America: namely, that race relations between American cultures, racial delineations within daily life, and realities and expectations based on race are getting worse, not getting better.

For example, police interactions with largely Black communities are dangerously taking shape in a pattern consistent with the worst of our past, not the best of our future. In Atlanta, a 90-year-old Black woman was killed in her home by police during a "botched drug raid", one where police officers ended up admitting to planting evidence and falsifying other information around the case. Just last week in Woonsocket, Rhode Island, 4 White police officers broke into the home of a 74-year-old Black woman without a search warrant and without criminal charges pending against the woman. The ensuing handcuffing and rough-housing of the resident prompted her to have a heart attack and incur a subsequent stay in the local ICU, even after the elderly woman – who was alone at home – complained of chest pain. All this while the officers covered up their badges (to prevent being identified) and left the premises during the woman's suffering.

Public school systems have re-segregated themselves in a de facto fashion over the past 15 years. Recent studies by leading researchers have shown that Americans with "ethnic-sounding" names are less likely to get job interviews and loan considerations upon first glance by those in decision-making capabilities. Institutionalized racism is very real in America, a problem only exacerbated by the economic tension throughout America and the polarizing nature of the first Black president with his policies. That doesn't even mention our collective lack of balance to address this reality with the courage to eliminate the problem and the emotional temperance to do so without false and overreaching allegations. The added element that makes race so explosive in America again is not the mistakenness of the NAACP with its recent actions or the actualized racism of a minority of tea partiers. Sadly, it is that in today's America, combined with our inability to address the problems courageously and truthfully without a heavy dose of rhetoric to glaze over the realities, we face comes this stinging truth:

Black America is rapidly losing the moral authority to hold up its end of race healing.

As more instances of Black-centric animosity – be it from the mindset of "justification" for retaliation during the Obama Era or merely a misunderstanding of history and contemporary times – come to surface, the more a greater portion of America believes there is a sense of equal footing in all aspects of America, primarily because Blacks in America recently have shown a growing propensity to enact inappropriate racial beliefs. The rue of racial hatred is what keeps the poison recycling throughout our nation. Regardless of where the anger starts, it ends up impacting all of our lives.

Unlike others, I do believe that there is yet another level – or several – for us to achieve as the melting pot society. Further, I believe that we are capable of doing so with grace and honor. Yet, in order to make this a reality, we must confront the truths about where we stand regarding race as a melting pot American culture – even as we continue to watch the NAACP stumble over racial situations, select Tea Partiers tumble out of leadership because of their racial repugnance, and noted national spokesmen misspeak about the misreported death of institutionalized racism in America. Courage gives us the ability to correct the issue as it is, not how it is reported or how it used to be years ago. Conviction allows us to be fair with all Americans so that no mislabeling occurs. Commonality – as Americans - should give us the confidence to use these opportunities to address this head-on before the nation gets turned on its head – yet again - because of all this.

Appeared in The Daily Caller, July 2010

Harvesting Strange Fruits

Instead of harvesting the societal fields of change sorely in need of attention in Black congressional districts across America, more members of the Congressional Black Caucus choose to pluck the low-hanging fruit of blaming the Tea Party for the political woes of the nation.

If the typical, urban-based Black voter was like an amateur farmer, she or he would probably look at the political landscape right now, seeing a field full of rhetoric that is ripe with plenty of all sorts of things that look nice and, because of appearances, could be sold to Americans everywhere – particularly other Black folks.

The attentive farmer, however, would probably know that the fields these days are growing crops that look pretty to the novice but don't do much for those looking for something of actual substance.

Kind of like looking at a field full of dandelions and treating it as a good crop when the harvest actually needs wheat for bread – and nutrition – for an increasingly starving population.

That sounds like how the Congressional Black Caucus is increasingly treating impoverished Black Americans in critical need of leadership and solutions from their entrenched elected officials. Instead of reaching for the best and brightest ideas among us to give the people what they truly need, the CBC seems to be settling in on the strategy of giving the people the low-hanging, shiny fruit of political blame complete with more rounds of victimhood and scare tactics.

And, frankly, that fruit has become rotten to the core.

At the same time that some members of the Congressional Black Congress would like to openly blame President Barack Obama for the lack of economic development and improvement within their districts under the first Black president, they also seem content to build up the Tea Party boogeyman for him to run against during the 2012 election season without holding him accountable at all for the past 4 years of ineffectiveness. Providing more irresponsible, loose-lipped hyperbole concerning the Tea Party instead of giving sound leadership (even if it means being unpopular at this point of time) only sells Black voters caught in the vice of gerrymandered congressional and local voting districts a convenient distraction away from the issues that strangle their communities. Further, it shields these politicians from an evident truth that now pokes its head out through the recent oft-repeated comments from Rep. Waters (D-CA), Rep. Wilson (D-FL), and Rep. Carlson (D-IN): that the Congressional Black Caucus has become more adept at leading Black voters in advancing outdated messaging campaigns about race and politics in America than they are in helping Black voters become more equal as partners in the rebuilding and advancement of America.

Sadly, the more that we need avant-garde, love-based, revolutionary leadership from these current elected officials, the more we get hateful, misinformed actions and statements from a group supposedly representing the "conscience of the Congress." Instead of holding all sides accountable – including a president whose administration cannot say the word "black" without saying the word "tie" afterwards and asking for a significant campaign donation from everyone in the room - this group seems hell-bent on blaming the racial models from the 1950s on the problems in Black America in the 21st century. Instead of working on partnerships between fellow Christians within church communities regardless of political affiliation, it is just simply easier to wish that conservatives go straight to hell so that the elected elite can continue holding onto status while the vast majority of their constituents attempt to hold on daily without much hope.

Just as loud as the ear-piercing catcalls concerning Tea Party racism are (when inappropriate and disproportionate), the sounds of silence when their voices are truly needed is deafening – perhaps even more so. When Black men stand up against the societal obstacles and stereotypes to be better fathers, most of these members prefer to give a minute of a speech instead of muscle behind a movement. When young Black people are physically, economically, or otherwise abused by older community members, many of these "leaders" are quick to tap-dance away from the issues to protect their friends and donors than they are to gain moral authority and cache, even at the risk of losing precious financial resources. The same people that often speak of the courage of the Civil Rights Movement from years ago now fail to exhibit the courage – or the willingness - to befriend a perceived foe for a common goal or lose comfort in order to command a positive change. With the challenges facing Blacks in America in 2011, it is truly easier to blame a boogeyman than it is to bolster a block – or a community, or a nation. When the CBC takes that stale stance instead of taking bold, visionary action, the questions about the organization rightfully yield forth.

If there is still value in having a Congressional Black Caucus in 2011 (which, by the way, I do believe that there could be extreme value in it), it is being mortgaged out to pay for the protection of a few condescending, misguided, and marginalized members of elite pockets of Black America in their efforts to keep their seats of privilege. Rather than looking at themselves as nurturers of the Dream at a time when the MLK Monument is now up in Washington, many of these "leaders" see themselves as the embodiment of the Dream, not realizing that they were never to be anything more than a humble step stool so that the least advantaged among America (Black, White, and other ethnicities) had a chance to reach for that Dream. As a result, what we get is an increased amount of bad apples parading around as something delicious, hoping that more Americans take another bite of the outdated poison that is once again ripping apart this nation. At a time when the enemy is death and decay, not Tea Partiers in Duluth and Des Moines, the yield we are receiving from the CBC is looking more suspect to the eye and bitter to the taste with each passing minute. Even as Rep. Carlson says that there are some that want to see us hanging from a tree, if Black America hangs its collective hat on that rhetoric going forward from here, we can hang up our hopes from turning our nation around anytime soon.

Appeared in The Chicago Defender (online), September 2010

Misguided Priorities while Fighting Misogyny

The Republican attack on the federal funding of Planned Parenthood is not an attack on Black women and minorities. It's merely a counterattack on the federally-funded onslaught against people of color.

Plenty of left-wing politicos and social activists have taken to the streets to denounce the House of Representatives recent vote to de-fund Planned Parenthood (http://www.politicsdaily.com/2011/02/19/planned-parenthood-defunding-family-plannings-not-a-gop-family/) in an effort to reduce the federal debt. Those that are worried about Americans in underprivileged areas (Planned Parenthood hot spots, often urban and usually ethnic in nature) not receiving the education on family planning should take heart: there should still be plenty of non-for-profit organizations (including churches and other community organizations) that have promoted the benefits of sexual education without offering the abortion services that lead to crippling socioeconomically-challenged areas.

And those worried about the ability of Planned Parenthood to sustain its abortion services without the infusion of federal tax dollars to promote both its shady history (http://www.blackgenocide.org/sanger.html) and its assorted current controversies (http://www.washingtontimes.com/news/2011/feb/1/video-shows-planned-parenthood-manager-aiding-pimp/) should also take note: as long as their offices are located in urban centers, there will be plenty of opportunities for Planned Parenthood to continue their practices, especially with Black abortion rates in places such as New York City (http://abclocal.go.com/wabc/story?section=news/local/new_york&id=7883827) as they are today.

Planned Parenthood advocates such as expert Dr. Willie Parker, a medical director at Planned Parenthood Metropolitan in Washington, D.C believe that "...a hit on Planned Parenthood really becomes a hit for African-American women..." (http://www.theroot.com/views/pence-amendment-passes-house-votes-defund-planned-parenthood?page=0,1). Others consider the Republicans' de-funding through passing Title X an attack on women that choose abortion as well as the practice of family planning (http://www.cnn.com/2011/US/02/23/new.york.billboard/index.html). Of course, those that are abortion providers or advocates in cities that have a population with over 50% of its residents being African-American – cities that find themselves with high ratios of Planned Parenthood facilities available – would feel this way. However, those within disadvantaged communities that argue for the return of federal funding for Planned Parenthood at a time when money for Pell Grants and other much-needed educational resources are being curtailed or completely cut (http://www.cnn.com/2011/US/02/23/new.york.billboard/index.html) must look in the mirror and answer the question: at a time of budgetary cuts, should the fight be for funding life-advancing opportunities for at-risk students in need of support or giving more support to an organization with a long and detailed history of disseminating the propaganda of death to our communities? If the choice is about federal financial support – not whether or not Planned Parenthood continues to exist (as they will, even without federal funding) – then what should we direct the money coming into our communities towards: perceived dire straits or advancing lifelong dreams?

President Obama set a bad precedent for choosing abortions over academics in 2009 by using one of his very first executive orders to fund overseas abortions services akin to what Planned Parenthood provides (http://www.cnn.com/2011/US/02/23/new.york.billboard/index.html) before eliminating funding to educate poor Black children in Washington, D.C. (http://www.youtube.com/watch?v=QnptHuh-

[wKs](link)) and funding to HBCUs (Historically Black Colleges and Universities) ([http://www.blackamericaweb.com/?q=articles/news/the_state_of_blac k_america_news/9229/1](http://www.blackamericaweb.com/?q=articles/news/the_state_of_black_america_news/9229/1)) later that year. The cry for reviving Planned Parenthood's stipend in for the Continuing Resolution in 2011 dangerously follows this harrowing path. Instead, the Black communities and those disadvantaged Americans in need of support should celebrate the Republicans' efforts on these issues, both on the DC Voucher program (http://www.cnsnews.com/news/article/boehner-introduces-bill-restore-dc-vouch) and particularly in the de-funding debate. At some point, the partisan banter that we as African-Americans take on regarding the abortion rights debate should not blind us to the ramifications impacting our future when precious resources find their way to aid dream-ending services instead of heading towards the best and brightest of our future.

At a time of economic and social crisis, our nation is not at a point to twiddle away dollars to organizations that do not have the best interests of our families – and notably, our women – in mind. Neither Planned Parenthood nor many others within the abortion-rights community of service providers provide an adequate picture of the psychological or physical damage done to Black women as a result of abortion, not to mention the less-discussed feelings of the fathers of these children that had little-to-no input on the decisions consummated at Planned Parenthood. As well, during a time when African-Americans struggle to unify to overcome community crisis in education (http://blogs.ajc.com/get-schooled-blog/2010/06/02/new-national-dropout-rates-25-percent-of-all-students-nearly-40-percent-of-black-and-hispanic-kids-fail-to-graduate-on-time/) and tragedies including incarceration rates (http://www.finalcall.com/artman/publish/article_4059.shtml), abortion providers fail to highlight the celebration of hate groups of the high abortion rates within the Black community (http://www.chimpout.com/forum/showthread.php?64318-Since-1973-

14.5-MILLION-Shitskins-Less-and-Counting-Support-Abortion),
especially revealing in the fight for equality as hate crimes
occurrences continue to rise.

Perhaps it is true that more Republicans should attempt to stay
out of the bedrooms of Americans and their subsequent decisions
concerning sexuality. Yet, perhaps, it is also true that American
tax dollars should remain out of the fray of that complicated
debate as well, especially as those dollars can be used towards
educating those in-need and walking among us today instead of
leading to the deference of dreams – and the ending of others –
through the mis-prioritizing our values and what we will fight for
as a community.

Final edited draft appeared in The Root, February 2011

Sins of the Father, Part 2: Why We Have to Act Now

I wish that I hadn't watched the Derrion Albert video.

I really wished I hadn't. It broke my heart and sickened my stomach simultaneously.

But, then again, I feel like God has called many of us to watch it, remember it, and burn it into our memories forever.

And then ask how the brutal beatings of two young Black men from Chicago can come for two different reasons but maybe, just maybe, their deaths could symbolize two different movements that will usher in change.

It is going on 50 years since the death of Emmett Till. The beating of this Chicago youth in 1955 was senseless, brutal, and tragic. The kidnapping and torture of this teenager symbolized the brutality and insanity that was SDT (Southern Domestic Terrorism) during the heyday of Jim Crow. To her credit, the late Mrs. Till forced America (and the world) to take a good look at what we yielded and tolerated in America. To her credit, it forced American (and the world) to look at the real-time effects of racial hatred and the consequences of tolerance and inactivity.

What Mrs. Till gave us in 1955, we receive via the Internet in 2009. Now, the vivid death of Derrion Albert – an honors student from the South Side of Chicago – gives us a chance to see the consequences of our inactivity and tolerance towards the continued destruction of our cities and urban residents due to drugs, crime, and lack of education. We get to see what continues to occur because of our underfunded efforts to fix our communities; (and no, it's more than money from the government – it's about underfunding of resources: time, materials, community members giving back, personal accountability from each of us to change this epidemic in our communities, etc.)

For young people, we get to see the horrible consequences of being in the wrong place and the wrong time – or of letting your guard down for one moment in a moment of crisis.

The question now comes: what do WE do about it? Are we going to rally as we did during the Civil Rights Movement after the Emmett Till murder and ensure that we can remove this latest scourge from the face of the earth? Do we protest and not stop until we get those changes, just as we did during the 1950s and 1960s, even as the murders of Emmett Till were not convicted of their crimes? Whereas a moment in time (or a series of moments, if you will) got us to protest, march, demand, and challenge in court, what have the continued senseless deaths prompted this generation to do?

When are we as Americans going to address the violence in our cities to a point where we end this reign of Black Urban Terrorism (BUT), just as we did with SDT? (Indeed, some could say that we need to deal with the BUT of the problem in our communities…) I know that my "Festive 40-Day Fast for the Future" (http://lennymcallister.com/news.php?item=97) was a step, but apparently not enough of a step to prevent something like this from happening. With the amount of rage and violence found in our communities must be a superior level of commitment, love, and wisdom to overcome this plague.

The sins of our fathers are yielding rotten fruit, folks. There is no other choice: We Have to Act Now.

Folks -

Stop waiting for teenagers and misguided youth to turn things around themselves. Stop blaming the misguided and the victims of this generation for its current conditions without engaging this generation towards the solutions. Stop thinking that it's someone else's problems or someone else's children. It's not. They're ours. It's enough. And it's now that we are going to step up.

Not have to step up. Will step up.

What's This Generation's Emmett Till's Moment?

What is going to be the occurrence that is so heinous that we as the emerging generations of Black Americans will never turn away from injustice and dysfunction again in our lifetimes? And must this injustice come in the form of white-on-black racism before we act?

One of the greatest things that an American did for us over the past 100 years is pull the wool from over our eyes, giving us a chance to see the depths of dysfunction and despair in the midst of her personal tragedy and grief.

Mamie Till kept the casket open in 1955 so that we did not have another opportunity to look away from the horrors that went on around us, using our own personal struggles and daily activities as convenient excuses to consider the social cancer epitomized by America's violent and racist tendencies as someone else's illness. As a result, many parts of America took notice, much of the world took umbrage to American hypocrisy resulting freedom and Jim Crow, and Black Americans took to the streets to reverse the injustices permeating throughout the nation.

What is that incident that will make us stare at the reality before us in an unfiltered fashion, something that will make us directly deal with the truth and act accordingly?

For those of us in Chicago, we thought it could have been the Derrion Albert incident, the mob murder heard around the world of an honors student.

For those living in New York City in the 1990s, it was probably thought to have been Abner Louima assault at the hands of police officers, a crime so brutal that it left Mr. Louima hospitalized for

2 months after being violated with a plunger as his assailant attempted to "…break a man down…"

For those living in Texas in 1998, it was believed to be the murder of James Byrd, Jr., a modern-day lynching where Mr. Byrd was decapitated after being dragged behind a moving vehicle for three miles.

For those living in my native Pittsburgh in the 1990s, it was thought to have been the Johnny Gammage tragedy, where the cousin of a Super Bowl Pittsburgh Steeler died at the hands of police officers in a "routine" traffic stop some 9 days after the infamous OJ Simpson verdict that ripped apart the nation racially.

And all of this happened over the course of the 20 years since the infamous Rodney King beating by LAPD officers, coupled with the Simi Valley verdict that set off riots around the United States.

For those of us outraged by the gang rape of a Cleveland, Texas 11-year-old, maybe we have finally arrived at that point in time.

Then again, maybe not. And that, my beloved, is downright scary.

Unlike 1955, we now live in a time of flash-forward news cycles and ultra-violent visual media, a time when desensitization of the American people to sex, crime, violence, and murder can all be epitomized in one video game; (has anyone seen "Grand Theft Auto"?) With all of the modern technology at our fingers, it is horrific to think that Emmett Till's battered and abused body – if shown to us initially in 2011 – would be nothing more than a curious object of a digital picture to tweet or email, leaving us disconnected to the actual meaning behind the unspoken message before our eyes.

Black people, wake up. Wake up now before it is too late. In fact, too late is already proverbially knocking on the door and playing with the keys, trying to take permanent residence in our lives.

If this incident in Cleveland, Texas – coupled with the scores of tragic and horrific incidents that we incur as a community on a regular basis over the course of these past 20 years – has not brought us (particularly the desensitized young (Black) generations of Generation X and Generation Y/Millennial Generation) to our present-day open casket to look down at the aftermath of apathy, backsliding, and civic (and social) decay, what will? The generations that rose up after the Emmett Till murder did not ask for current Black leadership to acquiesce to a collective response – they created it, one with a diverse set of approaches and remedies that sought a common goal: the acquisition of peace and equality.

It is going to take a lot of sacrifice – a lot of sacrifice. Sadly, the years removed from the work entailed in the Civil Rights Movement has allowed us to collectively forget the high levels of personal and professional danger, sacrifice, and isolation that people went through continuously in order to advance the nation significantly. No, we are not there completely despite the accomplishments of today's elder generation during their heyday several years ago. Therefore, it will take another level of selfless, perpetual activity to move forward with the next steps before us.

Our communities' issues with Black male dysfunction will not change until the **men** of our communities are willing to partake in a *years-long* endeavor to deal with the **males** within our communities until we can bring them along into manhood – including the older males that have been fighting that transition for decades now. Our communities' failure in the realms of unemployment and education will not be reversed until those with both proper education and employment bestow their insight on the lost. Those efforts – along with others that are much needed in Black America and, dare I say, throughout much of young America regardless of race – are efforts that must supersede our desire to wait until we "made it" economically before we act or our caution against "sacrificing too much" in the process of being a vocal, visible, and vociferous champion for a new social order within our communities. Believing that the collection of refreshed leadership must come from a legacy background (via family connection, college alumni base, or neighborhood upbringing) or from a particular status in life (via wealth, or professional status) will simply serve to keep us in the current African-American social cycle of "paralysis by analysis" or, more appropriately, "death despite dissertations." Folks, we are going to have to sacrifice items that make us more uncomfortable, vulnerable, fatigued, and secularly poorer than we are right now. People of affluence will have to sacrifice their earning potential at some point in order to invest the time and personal presence it will take to revamp our communities. People of modest means will have to step outside of the comfort zone to take on the prevailing injustices strangling our children in their social sleep. People in poverty will have to, once again, act like kings and queens. It will take all types of investment – building off of what is already in place yet taken to a higher level. Change of this magnitude in the Black communities of Chicago (and the nation) is not going to come without an actual, tangible taxing on our money, our minds, and our souls. Eliminating Jim Crow took a lot of focus but at least we had a legal common goal. Eradicating the self-hate and self-destruction within our communities will take a lot more self-discipline to do this self-healing.

The Rev. Al Sharpton once told me during one of my expressions of disgust with the current lack of young Black leadership that a social change does not need to come with the movement of the masses initially, but instead can be successful with the persistent actions of the dedicated few. I believe him, but I just wonder what it is going to take for those persistent, dedicated few to truly open our collective eyes, make us stare into the reality of today's Emmett Till Moment (and coffins), and deal with the reflection of what we see until we change the images we are looking at and shaping in our communities.

Appeared in The Chicago Defender (online), March 2011

The Meaning for the 4<u>th</u> of July for Today's...

Some would use the word "negro." Others would use terms such as "Black American" or "African-American." Regardless of choice, today's community must find its own special meaning this weekend amid the waves of patriotism and the speeches revering America.

Throughout the diversity of Americans, July 4th holds a wide range of meanings and expectations.

For some, the 4th will be nothing more than a well-deserved day off to cap off a much-needed 3-day weekend. For those here in Chicago, it is a symbol to remind us that the annual Taste of Chicago is coming to a close, complete with fireworks capping off the week-long activities.

For others, it will be an excuse to fire up the grill or crack up the refreshments in order to take in the weather and make the most of a summer day. The 4th becomes a good time for swimming and lounging, for making old acquaintances and remaking old recipes.

Of course, for politicians, pundits, and leaders, the 4th of July is a welcomed opportunity to give talks and speeches about the greatness of this nation. It is a time where men in power red ties and women with American flag lapel pins are able to captivate an audience by directing our attention to the proud history of our American forefathers regardless of race, creed, and socioeconomic lot in life. It is a time when the rhetoric of what America is supposed to be for its citizens – and, dare I say, for the world as an example of liberty and freedom – rings full bloom.

But, just as the great Frederick Douglass said so eloquently many decades ago with his famous speech "The Meaning of the 4th of July for the Negro" (a speech my father made us read as 8-year-old children after a visit to Douglass' home during a family summer trip over a July 4th weekend), we must be mindful – particularly in these times today – of the very specific and heightened meaning that the 4th of July should have for our current generations of Black people in America, the racial descendents of Frederick Douglass. For most of America will spend the 4th of July celebrating the victory of the American Revolution, we must collectively prepare and engage immediately in the fight of a revolution to recalibrate and reinvigorate urban America. If much of America will be caught up celebrating the tenets of American life and liberty, we must be captivated by the tough love task of preserving American life, notably the life of our youth that are being wasted. If much of America will celebrate its civic and geopolitical strength through the patriotic spill of blood and sacrifices of the past, we must gather together more strength immediately to stop the flow of blood rolling before our eyes everyday.

Our voices and actions must echo louder than a midsummer night's fireworks and our results must illuminate our path with a diversity of success within America once again, showing colors that cover the range of backgrounds that make this nation so unique.

Our frustration with the current conditions that are marked with the ebb and flow of tragedy and solace has been well documented. Yet, if the 4th of July is to signify celebratory times for most of America, it must signal to us that the time to elevate ourselves is now.

Who among us is tired of the shadow of death darkening the light of hope within urban America? Yet, who among us is willing to set down a tangible, measurable goal to track as we reverse the lifelessness within many neighborhoods? While much of the nation fills with talk of the American Dream on television sets and VFW halls this weekend, who is willing to dream another impossible dream within our communities? Who is willing to envision an American Dream where, say, 50% of the gang population is transformed within 14 years through a hybrid of education, employment, empowerment, and engagement with the rest of society? Who is willing to write down this task and keep us all accountable? Who is willing to speak up about this need for truth and change within our communities, even as other Americans give the typical talking points this weekend?

And if there are those that are willing to dream this obtainable yet daunting dream, who among us is willing to speak up and speak into existence this new reality? And if there are those that are already speaking this into existence – if their voices are merely a whisper in today's world as we are drowned out by American hypocrisy of equality in the midst of re-segregation throughout most of our American cities, who among us is willing to speak louder or perhaps shout? And for those that are already shouting, who among us is willing to stand up and ensure that you are both seen and heard for this change? And for those that are already standing up for the cause, who among us is willing to raise up others to stand with you?

As children from the finest schools in our land enjoy the summer holiday, how many of us will take to heart the vibrant symbolism of the 4th of July and ensure that the hollowness of the promise of educational equality for an increasing amount of Black children in 2011 becomes a distant and permanent memory within the course of a generation? Who among us is willing to sacrifice personally to create, pursue, and attain an educational goal that will re-route a large percentage of our youth from jail, dead-end jobs, and lifestyles of disappointment? Who is willing to dare say that we can uplift the collective grades within the Black community by a full letter grade within the course of 12 years? Who is willing to sober up Black America from the haze of tolerating high drop out rates by celebrating a thirst for knowledge within our youth more than our taste for forgetting our recent past with a good meal and a cold drink? Who is willing to see pharmacists where drug dealers presently roam? Who can look into the facts of 7th grade problem children today and see the vision of them being 70-year-old problem solvers down the road?

Further, who from within Generation X is willing to take up the mantle from leaders advanced in years and retired to the heavens, a mantle and mantra of remembering and reviving the belief that we come from a people that have done the impossible because we are a people born from a God of Infinite Possibilities? Who among the young are willing to save the youth? Those that have the most to celebrate this long 4th of July weekend are also the ones with the most to give as we endure the long, seemingly endless night of despair.

America may give in to its collective desire to hit the water, fire up the grill, and toast to another year of our national existence this July 4th, but in light of Douglass' original foil highlighting the differences for most Americans and Black people in the United States during his time, Black Americans today must be keenly aware of the call to make history at this moment in time, not sit around and reflect upon the joys of previous personal or national memories. The challenge this weekend for Negroes ranging from the Tea Party to progressive parties is pretty clear: we must avoid the hypocrisy of proclaiming freedom, the success of achieving true equality for all Americans, or the hope of political "good will" as a democratic society and instead take head-on the grim reality that a growing segment of young Americans are being reborn into slavery, shipped to the continents of Incarceration, Re-Segregation, and Mis-education, and left to rot in the concrete cotton fields of the modern ghettos of the United States. The meaning of this 4th of July for today's Negroes – at a time when Black unemployment is depressingly high, Black Americans collective health continues to decline, and intact Black families are becoming more of a myth than a mainstay – is not to be focused on political, social, economic, or religious labels more than we are on the perishing legacy that reeks due to our failure to act and our desire to act like the blind around us. The meaning of this 4th of July is that there is nothing to celebrate during these days. There is no leeway for a day off. There is no genuine naughtiness through accomplishments that deserves fireworks and a carefree attitude. There is too much work to be done and too few lovers of our people to be caught without focus for the duration of this year. And it starts with the acknowledgment that this 4th of July must be less of a holiday and more of a holy day within our communities – a holy day for rededicating ourselves to restoring our communities, just as leaders did before us.

On this 4th of July, when other Americans smile with pride as the flags wave and the rockets' red glare is above, it is time for us to finally taste the tears of the communities of Chicago and throughout our homeland. When others mourn the sacrifices that others made to make this nation what it is, a bitter taste should strike us with the repugnant thought that we are on the precipice of wasting the sacrifices of countless thousands that looked like us, many of who are nameless and faceless in the annuls of the cruelest parts of our history. When others kick back to take in the easiness of a paid day off from their jobs, we must get the message that it is truly time for us to get to work in a labor of love without a wage but surely with a price if we are not expedient and exceptional in our civic duties.

Much of America may rest on the laurels of the nation this weekend. Some of America may look to rebuild the nation starting this weekend. Black America must be about the business of resurrecting the nation – and notably our part of the nation – starting this weekend.

Appeared in The Chicago Defender (online), July 2011

The Obama PASS (Presidential Activism Selectively Shown)

Throughout his tenure, President Obama has been criticized for his passivity in speaking towards issues of race. Now, we see another instance of the president speaking up in an affair impacting Muslims. Should he get a pass from African-Americans for this inconsistency?

The silence from the White House – occupied by the first Black President of the United States – that we heard during the two Black History Months during his presidency were never as loud as they were on Friday evening.

President Obama's comments about the controversial mosque being built in Lower Manhattan that he gave during the Iftar dinner at the White House Friday blindsided a wide swath of Americans, notably Obama supporters. White House Press Secretary Robert Gibbs was one of them. He had spent the last several weeks avoiding the issue while fending off the media during repeated questions concerning the mosque. Another one of the blindsided many were at-risk Democrats on the campaign trail, those that are undoubtedly now dodged by voters that are emotionally stoked by this issue.

Among the blindsided that many are not talking about, however, are Obama's African-American supporters.

President Obama has taken a large amount of criticism over the past two years for his careful approaches to the issue of race as the first African-American commander-in-chief. Even in instances where those within his administration have noted the racial crossroads America sits at (e.g., Attorney General Eric Holder's initially-premature – but now increasingly pointed – remarks in February 2009 about us being a "nation of cowards" regarding issues of race), the president has been determined to stifle or otherwise segue conservation as quickly as possible. This is a very different approach than what President Obama has done towards the effort of Muslim awareness, outreach, and tolerance since becoming president – something that could make critics feel that Mr. Obama has is willing to show more of a public soft spot towards his Muslim background than towards his Black heritage.

Since 2009, President Obama has taken several controversial or ground-breaking steps in the name of creating a new relationship with and perspective on Muslims. He took this endeavor overseas to the Middle East in 2009 to address Israeli-Arab relations on the front lines. His administration had previously directed NASA initiatives to incorporate Muslim-friendly items into their pursuits. His recorded well-wishes to President Ahmadinejad after a potentially-corrupt election in Iran was ignored as the Iranians continued their march towards nuclear weaponry. Now, Friday's comments – ones that spoke directly in support of the mosque building built in Manhattan – exhibit another Obama moment where the president has been willing to uncomfortably stick his neck out in a controversy that has hurt allies, hindered American domestic peace, and helped tarnish his presidential legacy.

President Obama's actions influenced a chasm in the American-Israeli relationship seen earlier this year. They have also reignited the whispers from "birthers" about his legitimacy as president (as seen with the high-profile case of Lt. Col. Terry Lakin earlier this month).

His actions should also ignite a spark of cynicism within the Black community about President Obama.

During this same period of presidential Muslim activism, the Obama PASS (presidential activism selectively shown) has been flashed repeatedly to the African-American community by the White House with an explained-away stance on race that is both insulting and betraying. The president's refusal to dive deeply into matters that disproportionately impact Black Americans – from higher rates of unemployment to health disparities based on economics and education – has been an under-discussed regular occurrence during the Obama Presidency. This has occurred even as the administration has recently spoken out about the mosque in New York on behalf of Muslim-American rights in America and has sued for the appeal of SB 1070 in Arizona on behalf of rights for undocumented immigrants.

Out of a concern for being seen as a "Black" president, Mr. Obama has allowed excuses to be constructed that justify his failures to impact change in Black America, failures highlighted by in-fighting among Black conservatives and Obama supporters as well as media pundits including Tavis Smiley and the Rev. Al Sharpton. Conveniently, President Obama will scourge Black men on issues of parenthood and personal responsibility when addressing groups such as the NAACP to bolster mainstream and media support (ironically enough through leveraging a heavily-conservative message), but he also ignores the causes that contribute to many of the conditions plaguing Black America in the process. Actions including his 2009 move to cut the DC Voucher Program for disadvantaged Black youth and his prioritization to advocate for the 2016 Olympic Games in Chicago over speaking directly to the violence incurred by Black males in Chicago displayed Mr. Obama's continued willingness *not* to be identified with the African-American without his explicit hand in the process. However, I am certain that the president – along with targeted Democrats – will continue to take the 98% bloc of the African-American vote (a much-larger percentage of those Muslim-Americans that voted for him in 2008) in 2010 and 2012, even if the blatant unwillingness to speak out openly for Black people remains. Speaking to the equality granted to Muslims in building a mosque within

America can be understandable, but the president's willingness to speak on this matter should be particularly hurtful to Black folks in America due to Mr. Obama's constant unwillingness to speak on matters of race in the same manner – with conviction, passion, openness, and consistency – as he has on the Muslim perspective since becoming president.

In many ways, the Presidency of the United States is the ultimate bully pulpit, one that President Obama has used on several occasions to hammer home his viewpoints on Muslim-American relations within our borders and throughout the world. During a cold January afternoon in 2009, many African-Americans hoped that "hope and change" would also sweep in a use of the bully pulpit to finally address some of the most daunting disparities between Blacks and others Americans. It has not happened, perhaps in part because the president views the alliance of other minority groups as being more politically-expedient or potentially in-play. Regardless, Black America must kindly inform the president that Friday's comments (and his continued silence on matters of race) indicate that they have experienced the Obama PASS one too many times – something that will prompt a difference at the polls in November.

Final edited version appeared in The Root, August 2010

Drinking the Kool-Aid While Sipping the Tea

The Tea Party Convention this past weekend revealed the best of why Black America should pay attention but also the pitfalls that Black conservatives must avoid.

The Tea Party Movement is something that folks throughout Black America should be paying more attention to for a plethora of reasons.

I enjoy speaking at the parties. I enjoy meeting the people attending the parties. I agree with the overall principles of the parties.

They make sense for Black America.

The bonds between big government ethos and Black America need to be examined, threatened, and eventually broken if we are going to uplift our communities out of the mire seen in many urban environments since the implementation of the Great Society.

Getting government out of the way to allow small businesses to grow more will have a positive effect on Black America, thus providing avenues through which prosperity can filter into more African-American homes on a permanent and generational basis.

As I mentioned in the recent article in "The Grio" about the Tea Party Movement (http://www.thegrio.com/politics/some-blacks-back-tea-party-despite-movements-racist-reputation.php), we need to make sure that the talk surrounding the protests of the 21st century revolve around solutions that will allow a smaller government approach to take root and thus improve America. Political activism must link with community activism if we are going to lessen government spending and decrease the size of government.

211

Yet, as Black Tea Party activists – particularly during Black History Month – we also need to be mindful of our history and the overall impact of our participation if we are to improve America with our tea party participation. For every principle that we can espouse as tea party patriots (e.g., applying free market principles to schools and allow funding to follow the schools that provide the highest levels of *quality education* for our children as determined by college admissions, employment rates, and other proposed criteria), there are other ideas that we must be wary of and address.

One such idea? The call for a national "…civics, literacy test…" that must be passed before granting the right to vote.

Tea Party activists seemed to be in line with this idea and that, in turn, would seem to suggest that the African-American Tea Party activists would fall in line as well. I must say: I concur with their right to choose a position, and although I agree with the American tradition of free speech and respectful debate, I am moved to paraphrase the Reverend Jesse Jackson in response to this matter:

No self-respecting Black man should be in favor of imposing a "civics, literary test" to determine voting rights.

To supplement my statement, I ask:

What's next? A poll tax? A grandfather clause?

I know that there are some (hopefully not many) Black conservatives that agree that the former presidential candidate was not talking about Black people's suffrage because "…(m)ost of the people who vote are white…" but that "…if he were (talking about Black voters), I think it's a good thing that all voters have a basic literacy standard…"

It's too bad that any Black conservative would think this way. It's also Exhibit A – for alienation.

Those types of statements (cast in the obvious void of *recent* African-American history – we still have people alive that went through Jim Crow personally) serve as the epitome of why more African-Americans regard Black conservatives as the crazy cousins of the family – you know, the ones you let get in the family photo but you refuse to let say anything during Sunday dinner. Speaking and acting from a perspective that is separate from our *recent* history as African-Americans become self-explained illustrations as to why more Black people will not consider conservative policies and candidates or take Black conservatives seriously as potential leaders; (a sad reality considering that both dynamics are in need of change.)

Focusing more on getting true conservatives is appropriate for Black Tea Party activists. Losing focus on where we came from as a people while getting caught up in the rhetoric of the movement is inexcusable.

Americans have an ethical obligation to vote every election. People died for their right to be free and voice that freedom twice a year – every year. However, Americans also have a legal **choice** to vote every time and, further, they get to choose what issue or issues they want to vote on as well as their depth of knowledge about the issues. There is no requirement in the Constitution that forces people to be able to have a particular literacy, legacy, or monetary standard to meet in order to have access to voting.

That's why Jim Crow voting laws came into being roughly 150 years ago – the same sort of constitutionally-sidestepping maneuvers that Tea Party activists (including African-American activists) abhor currently from coast to coast.

And where Americans have the ethical obligation to remember the history enabling their voting freedom, African-Americans (including and particularly Tea Party activists) have a historical and moral obligation to remember the Black History that forged their voting history as well. Putting a literacy standard on a group of Americans that are already increasingly locked out of jobs, education, and quality standards of living via the achievement gaps in our nation only ensures that those individuals will continue to stay locked out – and America will continue to stay held back as a result. The "civics, literacy tests" to be enforced must not be done at the polling booths, but should be done at the dinner tables, classrooms, and social halls of Black America – places that could do better to see more African-American activists providing these inroads.

Increasing the civic education, awareness, and involvement of American voters in the system is admirable. Advocating that it be instituted as a legal standard for voting is un-American.

Any position from African-Americans– tea partiers or otherwise – that promotes putting standards on people that serve as gate-keeping mechanisms between citizens and their constitutional rights must be analyzed under the microscope of Black History and destroyed if the position is found wanton. There are certain positions and ideas that supersede party affiliation and philosophical considerations, particularly during a month where we celebrate the courage and accomplishments of the many that faced police attack dogs, violent Klansmen, and hidden snipers to provide the voting and other personal freedoms that we enjoy today as Black people. Anyone sipping the tea without taking a dose of reality along with it on this proposed issue of implementing standardized tests for voting access risks or displays the narrow-mindedness, self-centeredness, and disconnection with history that jeopardizes Black America as a dying sub-culture and inhibits America from reaching its fullest potential in the 21st century.

America – and Black America as well – is in need of a new political way. As a proud young conservative, I say that the Tea Party Movement is one way of accomplishing that way. However, we must ensure that we select the collective right way in doing that, from education and activism to politics and civics. If Black Tea Party activists get caught up measuring their equality in the movement while not keeping a historic eye measuring the African-American landscape, then it's only a matter of time before we have indeed lost our way.

Appeared in The Loop 21, February 2010

Cain, Conservatism and the Black Vote for 2012 and Beyond

No one wants to really go into why the conservative-leaning Black voter continues to line up staunching behind liberally-tilted Democrats without a glance towards the GOP. Beyond the cursory explanations.

Everyone wants to discuss the dynamics of racial politics in today's America, from explaining the complexities between Latino candidates and voters in 2012 to understanding whether Black voters will support President Obama as much in 2012 as they did in 2008.

Race still matters in America. We can not escape our original sin of the role of race in American society. Whether it is Dr. Michael Eric Dyson arguing the case for Republicans' apprehension for having a Black man in the Oval Office for another 4 years or discussions from various pundits with varying views on race and the ongoing Cain Train derailment, race has the uncanny potential to find itself in each aspect of our lives from politics to sports. Because it does, addressing specific voting blocs still makes a difference in general elections, even when the candidate himself downplays the role of race in American politics and society.

That downplayed reality, more than anything else at a time when Black America is falling into a sub-existence within America, is why leaving the question of the Black vote and conservative candidates so open-ended (or unchallenged) does both Black Republican candidates and the greater Black community a huge disservice politically.

Perhaps for the most part, Black America has subtly (or, according to some, loudly) answered the "Cain Black Voter Question" that was posed by the Washington Post. Despite what Cain supporters may say aloud, the hidden and quiet truth remains spoken, if by nothing else other than perception: Herman

Cain could not win a significant portion (e.g., 20%) of the overall Black vote in 2012, 9-9-9 and all.

Answering the Cain question still leaves the rudimentary issue of Black America and the Black conservative candidate relatively unsettled. Sure, we concluded that Cain could not get the Black vote in 2012 were he to become the Republican nominee, but why? Despite the high rates of unemployment in Black America over the past few years, the Reagan-esque (and coldly distant) comments from President Obama on his approach to helping Black America through the "rising tide" theory, and the incumbent's condescending remarks when addressing Black voters' frustration with his economic efforts so far, Cain's message still is not seen as resonating enough to make a difference.

The lesson learned by Mr. Cain, his supporters and, perhaps, Black conservative candidates that seek the Black vote is simply this: sharing melanin does not equate to sharing a common social understanding or political message.

Translation: if a candidate can't or won't speak to the Black vote directly, she or he will never get the Black vote if as a conservative.

Heck- that may be becoming increasingly true even if you are a Democrat. Looking at the wane of support and influence that the first Black president continues to incur is an example of this bearing out. At a time when more voters are looking for better results at a faster pace, they are less willing to jump patiently through hoops of incumbency and cronyism to see action from government. Black America, a segment of this nation in the most critical need collectively aside from Native Americans, needs direct accountability and relationship from their government at a time when racial disparities are widening. This approach contrasts greatly with "Cain-sian" viewpoint that many conservatives take: namely, that racism does not hold anyone back in today's America.

This clash in realities brings about the very obvious problem of getting Black voters to listen to Black conservatives on the campaign trial or within the political realm, primarily because a large segment of conservatives including leaders such as Mr. Cain are too quick to uphold their personal triumphs as paramount reasons why a cultural toxin is no longer relevant. Ignoring the realities of race in modern America or saying that we should all strive to be some unhyphenated American works within Tea Party factions or other parts of the conservative base. Yet, without also explaining to those same conservatives that small government realities will never take root successfully without fixing the issues that make big government necessary in mostly urban (i.e., Black) areas (e.g, bad schools, high crime, and low unemployment opportunities), the rhetoric is only useful for guest spots at events where Black conservatives work to alleviate the guilt and sting of the aftermath of racism.

When Black conservatives turn the corner on actively and collectively speaking to the Black community with a consistent sense of connection, brotherhood, and political sensibility, the Black community will begin to turn their attention towards Black Republican candidates – not a second sooner. Explaining the history of the Democratic Party or highlighting the plight of Black families since the Black vote swung to the Democrats proves to be informational. Building relationships with today's Black community with spirited compassion and sweat equity over political education will take the Black conservative dynamic in America to another level. Much of Black America wants to leverage conservative politics more often now in order to improve the well-being of their communities and families. Lately, the Democrats have not given these voters a reason not to defect from their progressive voting tendencies. However, Black conservatives – from Cain as a presidential candidate on down the ballot – cannot continue to address the incomplete answer of Black America and the Black conservative candidate with an incomplete effort in fostering genuine, tangible, and long-lasting partnerships that can bridge the nation over the troubled waters of today's America to a brighter future. Only with these conservatives going "all-in" can we get Black America to be all-inclusive with their political choices in 2012 and beyond for the sake of a better, more Perfect Union.

Appeared in Politic365, 2011

The Trayvon Gap Between Civil Rights Leaders and the Political Right

It's easy to allow the animus towards figures such as the Rev. Al Sharpton and others to color the opinion of Black leaders' active role in the Trayvon Martin case.

Ever since the Trayvon Martin case hit mainstream media with full force, the targets of frustration, mistrust, and outright racial hatred came out front and center in the minds of many Americans.

Tweets, Facebook messages, and comments at the water cooler echoed some of the same familiar opinions:

The Rev. Al Sharpton is race-baiting America once again.

President Obama is racially dividing the nation simply for the sake of his re-election bid.

Yes, these men have served as valid antagonists in conservative horror stories of the political left's agenda being advanced in America. At times, though, both have also been placed as convenient boogeymen by some, used collectively as a handy excuse to downplay racial issues or ignore legitimate concerns. They are accused of overextending their importance when speaking from their bully pulpits. Folks say that they are parlaying fear and mistrust to bolster their careers – and perhaps for some, even their bank accounts.

However, there are times when some Americans – and, sadly, many conservatives – refuse to admit or see the worthwhile role that figures such as Sharpton and Jackson have played in the ongoing toxin of race relation failures and its subsequent disparities they cause in America. It is as if many conservatives believe that calls for civil rights activism made by these two and many others (including people on both the political left and conservative right) are ineffective echoes from a distant past made by attention-hungry people causing more trouble than it's worth.

An example of why these conservatives would be wrong is the recent arrest of George Zimmerman in the Trayvon Martin case.

Sadly, many conservatives still have a hard time seeing the value in modern-day civil rights activism from Black political and civic leaders (on both sides of the aisle). There is a widening gap between conservative thought and effective, affable, and unifying legacies of leadership in an increasingly-diverse America.

Those that actively and openly abhor the presence of Rev. Sharpton and others in the Florida case seem to forget that without the public outrage nothing would have happened. Before that, the likelihood of anyone combing over the facts thoroughly – much less garnering an arrest for second-degree murder in a sketchy tragedy complete with overtones of stereotyping and overboard vigilantism – was slim and none. Those that inaccurately portray President Obama as some race-baiting politician using this case to his re-election advantage forget his famous diss of Attorney General Holder concerning race relations in 2009 or his "rising tide lifts all boats" statement concerning racial economic disparities. They fail to recall how President Obama was criticized by Black civic figures for being silent for too long on these types of issues. They also forget that all presidential candidates – including Republicans – were challenged to symbolize "Moral Compass-in-Chief" for a hurting nation in a manner reminiscent of Eisenhower, Kennedy, and a select group of past presidents.

Civil rights awareness, activism, and vision still have a much-needed place in America. Granted, much of the attention must be shifted towards urban-centric issues such as education and economic disparities to address today's plagues. Black-on-Black crime must be more of the focus instead of always being directed towards Black-versus-White issues, even though the racial disparities and increase in racial tension demands full attention throughout the spectrum. With this movement being vital to improve and strengthen America in the 21st century, there is a necessary role that conservatives must play in the process. That role cannot be one of disgust or animus.

Reacting to civil rights activists without an honest analysis as to whether their involvement in a situation is valid is nothing more than a shallow reaction to yet another stereotype. In the end, it limits the effectiveness of conservatives in their quest to "take back America." If conservatives – including and especially Black Republicans – maintain an elusive stance on race in America or continue a condescending and non-cooperative approach towards addressing our deep-rooted racial issues, not only will they continue to see the likes of Reverend Sharpton in both necessary and "questionable" roles, but the conditions prompting their appearances will further permeate throughout urban America.

The criticism of those such as Sharpton from the political right – even in the midst of just and successful activism as with the Martin case – is not reactive to over-aggressive liberalism in America. Sadly, much of it has to do with the growing chasm between modern-day conservatives and their historical roots as defenders of justice for all, regardless of color or creed.

Increasingly, a growing segment of conservatives miss the point. Leadership in today's America has nothing to do with ruling over a mixed bag of citizens with conservative mandates. It is about understanding and leading a diverse constituency to modern-day prosperity with convincing conservatism that wins the future and wins over our critics. Sometimes, "winning" includes partnering with – or, at the least, holding back criticism of – strange bedfellows when the cause is sound.

Looking Forward: Why I Stay Amalgamated - Politics as a Sport that Remains a Daily Game of Life or Death

It simply does not matter what angle one wants to approach 2012 from.

True, it's an election year. It's hard for any of us to miss that obvious reality. It is for me, between watching cable news, talking on the airwaves with fellow pundits, or walking around President Obama's neighborhood as a fellow Hyde Park resident.

Yet, 2012 is so much more, especially for anyone that chooses to be an advocate for the diverse people in today's America.

For a moment, just take it all in.

Take a look at – and get a true taste of – the horrifying Chicago violence that is overwhelming the potential in our communities and snuffing out the lives of our young people. Human capital lost. Expectations lowered. America weakened as a result, an impact from the epicenter of urban life USA that resonates out to the cornfields of this nation.

Take a listen to the conversations held within the political circles of the grassroots and professional levels over developments such as the recent Supreme Court rulings on Obamacare and Arizona immigration laws. That chatter doesn't even take into consideration the upcoming tension that is bound to crop up from other notable items, including the Court's next look at the legitimacy and necessity of Affirmation Action in today's America.

Speaking of tension: take in the tension, the anger, the frustration, and – dare I say – the hatred brewing throughout our country due to a bad economy, poor options for leadership, and

224

woeful choices for America regarding politics and related moves that impact our society moving forward. Each decision prompts a slew of angry remarks and a sprinkling (at the very least) of vile suggestions. No side of the political aisle or social argument is immune to this.

There are so many things going on. Therefore, as a Black man, a Republican, a child of God, a father, a husband, and an American – not necessarily in that order – it is absolutely necessary for me to remember that I must remain "amalgamated" as an advocate for the people that I love in this great nation, from my family and friends that I speak directly to regularly to my fellow Americans that I have yet to meet. I have no other choice but to take it all in, even if it sometimes comes at the price of my own career detriment, social reputation, or mere lack of physical rest. Advocating for the best of this diverse nation is a challenging endeavor in modern America, making it absolutely mandatory that embraces the love for people that it takes to serve and the knowledge of self that it needs to weather all storms that will come. It is a tireless pursuit to advocate for the people that I love – and advocate not only for the sake of highlighting gap areas in our national fabric that work to rip the country apart at the seams, but to begin the process of implementing solutions. Because it is, in fact, an on-going journey in this important walk that encompasses life-or-death so regularly, I have to stay involved in this political game. I feel as though I have no choice. I love my family, my friends, and the people of this nation – and dare I say, my fellow children of God – too much to do otherwise.

Because I am deeply engaging and analyzing this political game that currently plays out in the United States (a discourse of ideas, strategies, and maneuvers that result in next steps in the American experiment of republican democracy), I never forget that politics – especially today – is a sport that shows itself as a daily game of life or death.

That is particularly so for the people that I find myself speak up on behalf of.

It is very, very easy for participants in the political discourse playing out throughout America to forget the ramifications of their actions. It is too easy for those that advocate for smaller government to forget about the scores of Americans that have now grown up highly dependent upon government assistance in multiple facets of their lives. These Americans currently need and, for the short-term future, will continue to need an active hand from grassroots Americans to root them out of that depressing cycle if smaller government, free market principles are embraced more within urban America. It is too easy for those that advocate for government intervention at all levels of citizen life to forget that their banter concerning government interaction and taxation has a real-life impact on the thousands of Americans living in places such as Fargo, North Dakota and Ames, Iowa – places that will never understand the plight faced by residents south of the Midway Plaisance in Chicago but know that continued government regulation and taxes to aid big-city dwellers can hurt them in small town USA.

In taking a more amalgamated approach in touting the perspectives purported today, we choose to be more aware of the complex problem set we face, the awesome potential we have in this nation, and the great responsibility we have to get this right – aside from the entertaining yet oft-separating discourse we share today.

In the depths of discussions on public radio and cable television, there is plenty of room for talking heads and politicians alike to rumble with each other and forget that the competition of ideas that takes place everyday in front of the national audience is not a debate for the sake of winning arguments or even for the sake of winning the hearts, minds, and voters of potential constituents. In actuality, the political competition engaged by thousands each day is only supposed to be won for the sole purpose of staying on the side of life over death for the sake of Americans everywhere.

That's all that there is to it. Any other effort that slides outside of the scope of this simple metric works outside of the realm of advocating for a better America and finds its task – in one way or another – with a motive that is more self-centered than one may care to admit.

That doesn't make people bad for going down this path. There are often plenty of good reasons to be a little self-centered, from caring about family and "primary constituents" to working towards career goals. Admission of this reality does our communities throughout the nation good overall. Knowing that there are specialized advocates that are focused on an exclusive group or small set of outcomes does not harm the system as long as there remains an identification and understanding of those playing this role in the system. However, to be a successful amalgamated advocate in today's America, it is darn near impossible to approach any of the political competitions that occur daily – from debates in social media arenas such as Twitter and Facebook to the always-engaging GOP vs. Dem debates on cable television – and have ulterior motives. Yet, over the course of the past few years, it is clear yet sad that there are plenty of people in this nation that claim to advocate for all Americans, only to speak out on behalf of a select few, hoping to drown out their ideological foes with rants and tear-downs that end up having a detrimental effect on the nation.

Competition – whether it is within free markets for businesses or on the athletic fields of the Olympic games – elevates quality. Political competition, therefore, should elevate the quality of life of the people that it touches. In essence, the game of life or death that is played out each day on the political battlefields of the USA should, as its primary yield, provide better opportunities, solutions, and results for the American people it touches.

I know that I am not the only one that views competition – and today's ongoing political competition – in this manner. Yet, at the same time, I know that there are plenty of people (and perhaps plenty more people, in fact) that will tell me that this view of politics is a little altruistic or naïve.

Maybe so, but to be fair in illustrating my point: if politics (as from the Greek word *politikos*, meaning "of, for, or relating to citizens") is about people ... and the salaries of those working in politics comes from said people (directly or indirectly)...and the audience of those in the media and entertainment sides of politics is made up of these same people...

...shouldn't the actions undertaken at the most important levels of politics – the legislative and representative roles of government, the think tanks and media megaphone aspects of the discourse, and the grassroots organizations on both sides of political thought – reflect an altruistic attitude concerning any actions undertaken within the various levels of political hierarchy today? Shouldn't the words, thoughts, and activities (both public and informal) of more people within the political process – including those that are merely involved via their vote – accentuate a notion that politics can still be about people or, if necessary due to a chasm, our collective actions should be about bringing politics back to the people? Shouldn't public activism and political advocacy have more of a hold on this mindset?

And, of course, as a formerly young but still proud young conservative, can't we accomplish these things as Republicans in the 21st century, at Tea Parties, within general assemblies throughout the states, and with new social and political partners in this melting pot country of ours?

Of course, as an amalgamated advocate, I say yes with my words, actions, and – needless to say – this book. Further, I think that it is necessary to embrace this approach if we are to be effective advocates in this changing nation.

Perhaps we all at some point fall short of the political mountaintop in the same manner that we all fall short of the glory of God as His children on earth. There are times when our deeds – verbal, written, or enacted – do not fulfill the best that we can be. With that said, one's intent becomes key in this whole process of being an effective advocate for today's America, particularly as we start to regularly hone in on the fact that politics is nothing more than one of the most important national arenas where life or death is played out on a very regular and very real basis.

I only do what I do because the struggling in our nation need another type of voice. There are enough legacy politicians, wealthy socialites, political ideologues, and 'perfect people' in the process already. I know that I'm not perfect, but in these imperfect times, We the People sometimes need imperfect peers to lead together in Order to form a more perfect Union. Because I'm not perfect, I get afraid but do not fear. Because I'm not legacy, I shake hands with commissioners and congressmen yet share kindred with custodians and meat-cutters. Because I'm not rich, I may struggle on my journey but I will always work for a better path for struggling neighbors and the American Way of Life. What's the use of my struggles if I do not give life to the voice of others that struggle as well? Why speak out if I don't want to serve others? Why serve if I don't want others to succeed? Why get on the national stage if I won't speak out so more Americans can get ahead? Not everyone has a chance to lift one's voice and speak out, but if those that have that chance speak out with honor, insight, and courage, everyone will have a voice after all.

That is why I do all that I can NOT to shy away from diversity. Instead, it is of utmost importance to embrace it and articulate it in a way that allows me to speak out in a holistic fashion, one that allows my perspectives to make the most sense even when others disagree with me. That is why it is important for me to show exactly how and why I am "amalgamated". If Tea Party principles and big-city plight cannot find common ground where both can co-exist, work together, and succeed as partners, then the back-and-forth that currently goes on between the two sides will only remain a competition for the attention of the media or votes in November instead of being a competition that truly elevates the quality of American life of all involved. If poor, urban conservatives cannot find kindred with well-to-do Republicans in the annuls of government while jointly seeking right-leaning leadership that will benefit our communities from the grassroots to our general assemblies, we are no longer talking about one mighty nation that is symbolized as the democratic melting pot. At that point, we are talking about a fragmented world power on its way to over-the-hill status due to our inability to fully grasp what's at stake in our daily political interactions and what's hidden within the power within our diversity of perspectives.

I believe fully that the best advocates in America today must ensure that they keep a bevy of perspectives in mind when engaging today's America and the problems we face. The reality is: without embracing the exponentially-spending nuisances in this rapidly-moving 21st century USA – or at least acknowledging them during our political discourse and public advocacy – we risk failure before we even begin our strongest and best-laid efforts.

That is why it is effortless for me to continue to refer to "Black America", despite the fact that the term burns up a lot of my conservative peers. Simply put, as long as Black Americans continue to experience such a vastly different reality from what most of my conservative brethren live on a daily basis – experiences often occurring as a result of the life-or-death game of politics played out by political representatives on the behalf of their oft-unaware constituents - – I understand that we are not speaking of an amalgamated section of fellow Americans. Therefore, it is separate and, from its practical reality, not the same America that others live in. Because of that, I know that as an advocate of my loved ones in today's America, I am one of the bridges tying the two together. Through words and actions that illustrate the chasm between the two can I articulate the problems with the widening gaps between parties that need each other in order to create and support a dominant 21st century America.

Just as well, it is easy for me to refer to Tea Party conservatives and establishment Republicans in the same breath as separate factions, although many of my progressive and liberal friends really do not believe that there is much of a difference between the two camps. Yet, anyone that has paid attention to the contention that has brewed between the grassroots of conservative thought and the entrenched structures of the Republican Party over the past few years understands that, even in the struggle to defeat Democrats in office, there is stinging interaction between the two. If these two sets of conservatives cannot find common ground in legislative maneuvers that engage their constituents in crisis – and perhaps even Democrats in power in the process - then we are not talking about an optimally-functioning political mechanism capable of serving people in the best ways possible. It really is that simple. If Black voters cannot trust conservative activists or if grassroots Americans cannot work with professional politicians, then we will continue to slide down the mountain from being the city on the hill to being a common town in the valley of despair.

Amalgamated advocacy must be smart, insight, and influencing – even without being compromising.

To be an advocate, it all goes back to doing the very best to serve people where they are with what they need to get them to where they need to go – and where we need our nation to head towards collectively.

In a nation as diverse, as large, and as powerful with kinetic and unfulfilled potential as the United States of America is, there is no room for both the entrenched and up-and-coming levels of leadership – be they elected officials, public figures, or grassroots activists - to ignore the need to take a more integrated and holistic approach to public service. That does not mean that conservatives could or should put down their political philosophies, nor does it mean that we should take a softer approach regarding the political competition of ideas that prompts the life-or-death interactions guiding so many lives on a regular basis in America. Rather, this task...this choice...this obligation, if you will...to take a more amalgamated approach to our roles as conservative advocates in today's America simply means that we have a higher obligation to articulate our ideas better, to inspire our audiences more effectively, and to advance our ideas beyond our comfort zones and established constituencies to date.

If we are the leaders that we say we are – or, to steal an infamous line from President Obama: "...we are the change that we have been waiting for..." - our conservatism cannot be a platform for merely getting enough independents to the polls come November or turn out enough conservatives to win down-ticket races in the fall. We have to act within the realms of the political game with a heightened urgency and acknowledgment that we are the individuals that must change the dynamics that hinder American advancement in the fields of economics, business, education, and social harmony. If we take to heart the belief that the sum of who we are as conservatives is just as important as the conservative values we purport, we will be more effective in influencing Americans and affecting voters, specifically those outside of our circles as we speak.

The political game is elevated in its grandest sense and to its greatest potential when we discontinue making sport of the historic obligations – and very specific current obligations - that conservatives hold in these times, an era that witnesses the failures of liberal policies throughout urban America, the results of Republican abandonment of the ethnic and urban vote for 40 years, and the disconnect created through our collective inabilities (or unwillingness) to embrace all sides and resources available to us to make the nation stronger and better. An advocate – even a good one – can identify with being a Black man or a conservative. A truly amalgamated advocate in today's America will make sure that he is never incapable of advocating for both sides without offending either side, even if disagreement in some areas ensues. An advocate in today's America can support pro-life positions or advance equality and respect for American women. A truly amalgamated advocate will be forthright and kind-hearted in extolling pro-life principles while articulating a level of tenderness and empathy for the unique needs of women in all situations, including those that may prompt political disagreements. An advocate in today's America may take a strong stance in immigration issues or stand up against bigotry against Spanish-speaking residents in America. An amalgamated advocate will find the way to allow both beliefs to permeate through one's words and actions without betraying any position. An advocate in today's America can relate to one region of the country over another and allow that emotional tie to be the love that drives her or his activism. A truly amalgamated advocate in today's America understands the beauty in this statement: from Cheyenne to Chicago, there is no such thing as "being in the middle of nowhere" or "being in the middle of urban hell", because within all corners of this nation exist the joy of Americanism and the presence of God's blessings on this rich and prosperous nation. They understand the kindred from the hills of the Ozarks to the coasts of both oceans our nation touches. The challenge that I find myself tackling everyday in my daily journey – as a child of God, a Black Republican, an urban conservative, and a community activist from a different elk, among other things – is the same one that I am asking you to take on yourself moving forward: find the best ways to approach and advance your positions in the daily political competitions. Engage the daily games of life-and-death that play out for Americans via the political process in a manner that amalgamates all of who you are. Do not relinquish your independent womanhood because you are a devout Christian conservative. Find the way to authentically make those traits within you co-exist in your political life for the best of America through your activism. Do not relinquish various traits as a member of Generation X or Generation Y just because you are a Young Republican. Those traits are necessary in the development of our political moxie, our social leadership, and our capability to write good laws when needed and identify - then repeal - bad laws when required. Find a way to allow all that you are to exude itself appropriately in your political life, doing so in a way that advances the competition of ideas that makes the American Way of government – our model of democracy – a beacon for other nations to behold and copy proudly for generations to come.

With the stakes so high in today's America, I cannot stress enough that amalgamation is not compromise. It is not weakness – it is strength. It is not watering down your values – it is understanding yourself enough to empower your values even more. It is not undercutting your positions – it is actually bolstering your validity through a higher sense of self and a deeper connection to more Americans. It is time – for the sake of 21st century America – for us all to begin speaking out more with our inclusive inner truths coming through in us as amalgamated advocates and activists (particularly grassroots and conservative activists). Those aspects, when articulated in a clear and combined fashion, build the bridges that can unite what is now a disjointed nation. This coming together of the different aspects of our personal activism symbolizes what we can do as amalgamated activists (particularly 21st century conservatives) and diverse Americans once we decide to embrace more of who we are in the political competition. This refining of our definition of who we are – and what we will do as a result - helps us to improve what we are as a nation and subsequently pursue the development areas necessary for moving forward successfully. The hidden potential of our nation today lays in the hidden truths in all of what we are and our abilities to leverage it successfully. Political pigeon-holing runs the risk of making our nation full of political bird-brains that define political discourse as nothing more than having a squawking competition. With the challenges before us and the mistrust among us, finding our truths and embracing the opportunities given through amalgamated advocacy – less a focus on national diversity than an understanding and utilization of interpersonal diversity in the expression of one's politics – is key. It is a powerful and viable way to not only begin to understand ourselves better, but it is the way to better understand our nation as we exist today while knowing how best to apply our political principles and arguments to serve today's America with the historic framework in mind. It is about winning the day – not for the sake of winning a media segment or a local election today, but for the sake of winning back this era so a stronger America can rise from the ashes of a nation that is hurting and increasingly hopeless. That is our task as advocates in today's America: winning the political daily game of life-and-death with a primary focus on winning back America...a more proficient, more robust, and more capable America...one day at a time...with amalgamated, astute, and inspiring advocates that understand that embracing more of self in a truthful way can lead to embracing the truth hidden without us: that America still has everything it needs to lead and succeed. I believe. I am thankful that you do as well.

Special Thank Yous to

My God
My ace
Alicia
Peace
Babykins
My family
TJ
My LS
My prayer group
My new team
My old homies
My loved ones at WVON
My folks at Chicago Public Radio and Vocalo
CNN
My drivers at 2:30 AM for Early Start and other Mornings
TYT
BET
TV One
Cliff Kelley
Malcolm
Toyia
My peeps in the NC
My people in the DC
Twitter-verse followers and friends
My Facebook friends and family
And the many that helped me along the way that I cannot list for fear of running out of space...

Thank you all. God Bless you always.
TCNGB (Take Care N God Bless)

www.ingramcontent.com/pod-product-compliance
Lightning Source LLC
Chambersburg PA
CBHW070001300526
45794CB00001B/144